Level Up Your Social Life: The Gamer's Guide To Social Success

By Daniel Wendler

Contents

If you are afraid, come forth.
If you are alone, come forth now.
Everybody here has loved and lost
So level up and love again

Call it any name you need.
Call it your 2.0, your rebirth, whatever—
So long as you can feel it all,
So long as all your doors are flung wide.
Call it your day #1 in the rest of forever.

If you are afraid
Give more
If you are alive
Give more now
Everybody here has seams and scars
So what. LEVEL UP.

—Vienna Teng, Level Up, from the album Aims
©2013 Soltruna Music www.viennateng.com

How To Use This Book

I know you're anxious to jump into the guide itself, but take two minutes to read this section first. Everything will make much more sense if you do.

This guide is organized into three stages. Each stage has seven levels, and each level has one main quest and three side quests. (There are also some bonus appendixes because everyone likes bonuses.)

The Stages

The stages divide the book into three different section, each focusing on a different goal. The stages are an easy way of tracking your progress, as well as telling you the "big idea" I'm trying to address in each part of the book.

The first stage, "Character Creation" focuses on changing your habits and routines. You'll be changing your life in little ways—like being more social, more open to experience, and more willing to take risks. The goal is to make you more naturally social, by making social connection part of your everyday life.

The second stage, "Multiplayer" is all about conversation skills. You'll learn how to have successful conversations, how to read body language, and how to connect with others.

The third stage, "Looking For Group", is about building friendships and going deeper with friends. The focus here is on building in-depth relationships—making new friends, getting closer with the friends that you've got, and feeling more connected with others.

The stages are designed to be completed in order. Character Creation prepares you for Multiplayer, which prepares you to succeed when you start Looking For Group.

Levels

Levels are basically mini-chapters. In each level, I'll talk about how a concept from gaming can help you improve your social life. Then I'll give you a main quest and some side quests to help you practice what you learned.

Main Quests

Each level has a main quest for you to complete. Quests are a way for you to apply ideas from the book to your life. Much as you complete quests in RPGs to make your character more powerful, you'll complete these quests to make yourself more social.

Each quest includes:

- The quest objectives (what you do)
- The quest description (how you do it)
- The quest rewards (why you should do it.)

There are three kinds of quests.

- Collection Quests: Do something a certain number of times.
- Daily Quests: Do something once a day for a week.
- Weekly Quests: Do something once a week for a month.

Feel free to tweak this if you want. If once a week seems too difficult, try every other week. If you want faster progress, try twice a week. If you really like a quest, do it over and over.

The most important thing is to pick a pace that you can stick with. The goal is to move fast enough that you're making progress, but slow enough that you don't feel overwhelmed.

Side Quests

Each level has three side quests. Side quests are bonus challenges, and each one is different. They might give you an extra opportunity to practice, make the main quest more challenging, or introduce you to the games I talk about in the level. Side quests are totally optional, but you'll get more out of the guide if you do them. I recommend doing at least one per level, and it's great if you can do all three.

Appendixes

At the end of the book are three appendixes: Cheat Codes, Achievements, and Game Directory. Cheat Codes has quick tips and tricks that you can use in social settings, Achievements are tongue-in-cheek awards for using this book, and Game Directory shows you where you can play every game I mention in this book.

Quest Strategy Guide

In some video games you can level up just by reading a book, but real life doesn't work that way. In real life, you need to practice if you want to get better at something.

That's what the quests are for. The more quests you complete, the faster you'll reach your social goals.

But be careful. If you start too many quests at once, you'll be overwhelmed. If you start quests too slowly, you won't make much progress.

To strike the right balance, I recommend the following strategy:

- Start a new collection quest when you finish the last collection quest
- Start a new daily quest each week
- Start a new weekly quest every other week (so you should have two active each month.)

In other words, you should usually be working on one collection quest, one daily quest, and two weekly quests at a time. That's four quests total, which is challenging but doable.

Of course, this is just a rule of thumb. You might find that you prefer to do more or less at a time. Or you might find that you can do a lot of easy quests at once, but need to slow down when a hard quest comes along. If you feel challenged but confident you can handle it, you're probably doing the right amount. Basically, think of it like the difficulty setting on a video game—if you're getting creamed, make it easier. If you're sailing through without a challenge, make it harder.

You should also try to track your quest progress. It's a hassle, but if you track your progress, you're much more likely to succeed. A few options for tracking quests:

- Pen and paper (especially if you tape it up somewhere you see it every day)
- A spreadsheet
- Todoist.com
- HabitRPG.com

I recommend setting aside a certain time each day for updating your quest progress. For instance, you might give yourself five minutes during breakfast or dinner to review your current quests, update your progress, and perhaps re-read a tip from the guide. This might sound like a lot of work, but once it becomes a habit it will feel effortless. Plus, daily checkups will make you much more likely to success with your social goals.

Stage One: Character Creation

Level One
Press Start

This is not going to be easy.

I'm going to ask you to change. I'm going to ask you to grow. I'm going to ask you to fail, again and again until you learn to succeed.

But I promise you, it will be worth it.

It was for me.

When I was growing up, I was the nerdiest, most awkward kid you could ever hope to meet. My comfort zone began and ended with my Super Nintendo, and my social abilities were limited to 1) talking about Star Wars 2) talking about video games and 3) talking about Star Wars video games.

In high school, I was diagnosed with Asperger's syndrome, a condition that makes it much harder for me to learn social skills naturally. So I decided to learn them deliberately, like I was studying a foreign language. At that point, it was about survival more than anything. I just wanted to stop the teasing.

But I was dreaming too small.

Learning how to be social is far, far more than avoiding bullies. It's about giving your life more meaning. The memories that matter the most to me are not boss battles or high scores. They're memories of people. I remember late night conversations, dinners with a table full of friends, and incredible dates that ended with kisses in the rain.

I think everyone deserves those kinds of memories. I think everyone deserves a place where they belong, close friends who know them deeply, and the confidence to put their best foot forward in new social settings.

And I wrote this guide to help you get there.

Here's what I need you to do

Quest 1.1 (Type: Daily)

Quest Objectives

- Open the book every day this week.
- Yes, that's really it.

Quest Description:

Most people quit.

This quest is about making sure that you don't.

Here's the thing. Being more social is not rocket science, and it's not magic. Like most skills, if you work at it a little bit every day, over time you will get a lot better. The key is just making sure that you work at it a little bit every day—without giving up!

So here's your quest.

Open this book tomorrow, and then keep opening it every day for a week. You can read it for five minutes. You can read it for an hour. You can even just skim the table of contents if you really want

Here's why. If you want to succeed socially, you need consistency. You need to let social growth be a regular part of your daily life. Most MMOs keep user interest with daily quests—you've got to log in at least for a few minutes to finish the daily quests. You need to have the same kind of consistency with your social life.

Obviously, it's not the end of the world if you skip a day. But if that skipped day turns into a skipped week and then a skipped month, you're in trouble. That's why it's so important for you to practice consistency.

So your first quest is simple: Read this book every day this week. Of course, you can keep reading today. But I want you to commit that you'll pick up the book for the rest of the week too. Think you're up to the challenge?

Quest Reward:

- A higher chance of completing the book

- Better odds of achieving social success

- The rest of the book is super cool and you don't want to miss out.

Side Quests:

- Raise the stakes. Get seven five dollar bills, and stick them somewhere out of the way. Every day that you pick up this book, grab one of the five-dollar bills and use it to treat yourself to something fun. Every day you don't read, grab a bill and make a $5 donation to charity—or if you really want to motivate yourself, just shred it.

- Write down three concrete, vivid goals. Imagine three specific, vivid goals, and write them down. Don't pick abstract ideas like "I want to be more social." Choose goals like "I want to be able to start a conversation with someone else and have it go well" or "I want to host a movie night for at least three other people."

- Schedule time to read. Choose a specific time tomorrow when you'll pick up the guide again—and set a reminder!

Level Two
Random Encounters

One of the most enduring tropes of RPGs is the random encounter. Want to make your character stronger? Walk outside of town until you run into a random monster, bash the monster over the head until it falls over, and then move on to the next monster.

The implications of random encounters don't make much sense (how does anyone get anything done when monsters attack them every ten steps?) But the basic logic is sound: If your character does a lot of little fights, they'll be prepared to handle the big boss fight when it rolls around.

And the same logic is true when it comes to social interactions. Obviously, there are some differences—please don't bash random people over the head! But the big idea is the same. If you make the most of all of the little opportunities to be social each day, you'll feel much more confident in high-stakes social situations.

Unless you never leave the house, you probably have dozens of little opportunities to be social. Whether it's the cashier at the store, or the person sitting next to you in class, or the coworker you work with, you have the opportunity to connect with several people each week.

The thing is, most people waste these opportunities.

Most people go through life treating others like NPCs, not like real people.

See, when most people interact with strangers and acquaintances, they generally connect with them on a functional level, not a personal level. Connecting with someone on a functional level means you interact with them only enough to accomplish a particular function. For instance, you talk to the cashier just enough to check out. You talk with a coworker just enough to get information on a new project. When you add social pleasantries (like asking "how are you doing?") you only add enough to accomplish the function of conforming to social norms.

Connecting with someone on a personal level means that you treat them as a person, not an NPC. It means recognizing that they exist outside of their interaction with you, and trying to show some interest in them or a little compassion towards them.

Practically, it might look like telling your cashier you appreciate their hard work. It might look like asking a barista what her favorite coffee is. It might look like asking your coworker about his weekend. It might look like asking a classmate how he did on the last test. It could just mean giving someone eye contact and a genuine smile. It might be looking at a name tag and saying "Thank you, [Name]."

It isn't that hard to do, but it can make someone else's day. And it can supercharge your social confidence. Instead of remembering the times you failed socially, you can think about the dozens of little moments of connection you had throughout the week. Instead of relying on rusty skills to connect with a new friend, you can use abilities that you practice constantly. All it takes is a deliberate choice to treat the other person as a human instead of a tool—a fellow player, instead of a disposable NPC.

That's what today's quest is all about.

Quest 1.2 (Type: Collection)

Quest Objectives:

- Create 10 moments of connection with strangers or acquaintances.

Quest Description:

This might feel a little awkward at first. And you might screw up. You might ask a question that's a little too personal, or p try to start a conversation with someone who wants to be left alone.

But that's okay. Stick with it, and you'll find you succeed more than you fail. And I think you'll also find that these moments of connection feel great, for both you and the other person.

Of course, having a social life means more than connecting with random people. But we're laying the groundwork here. Remember, random encounters prepare RPG heroes for the boss battle. Every time you deliberately create moments of connection, you're getting a little more confident socially, and a little bit better at relating to others.

Quest Reward:

- Start a habit of connecting with others
- Practice your connection skills
- Make ten people feel a bit happier.

Side Quests:

- Don't stop at making moments of connection with strangers and acquaintances—create some with family or friends, too!
- When someone creates a moment of connection with you, notice what they did that made you feel connected with. Then do that with someone else!

- Create a few moments of connection online. Send a friend an email just to say hi, or to thank them for something they've done for you.

Level Three
Leave the Starting Zone

Most games have some kind of starting zone for new players.

First person shooters often begin with a tutorial of some kind. MMORPGs have a newbie zone where the monsters don't attack you without provocation. In the starting zone, things are easy, and it's very unlikely that you'll fail.

Of course, if you never leave the starting zone, you miss out on most of the game. Leaving the tutorial means you'll probably end up dying a few times, but it also means you get far more enjoyment.

In real life, we've got something like the starting zone—it's your comfort zone. Your comfort zone is the conversation topics you've already discussed many times before. It's the activities you've already experienced. It's the people you've already gotten to know.

There's nothing wrong with the things in your comfort zone. It's awesome to have favorite hobbies and people you feel really comfortable with. But your comfort zone is limited. There is, so much that life has to offer. And if you stick only with what's comfortable, you'll miss out.

So today's quest is about expanding your comfort zone.

Quest 1.3 (Type: Collection)

Quest Objective:

- Find something you've never done before.
- And then go do it.
- (Optional) Go do it again!

Quest Description:

Pick something meaningful. It's not very meaningful to watch a Youtube video you've never watched before. It's much more meaningful to try yoga, explore a park near your house for the first time, or volunteer at a soup kitchen.

In general, you should feel a little nervous—if you are totally calm, you're probably still within your comfort zone. You might try asking yourself "On a scale of 1 to 10, where 10 is as scary as possible and 1 is not scary at all, how scary is this?" You probably want to try things that are in the 4-6 range on that scale.

That being said, the thing you pick should be something you actually want to do. It's good if it feels scary or hard, but it's not good if it just feels unpleasant. The point is to find an experience that will be rewarding, not something that is miserable. So if you know you'll hate the opera, don't choose an opera visit as your comfort zone expander.

Some possible ideas:

- Visit a local museum
- Go to the bookstore or library and read the first chapter of a book from a genre you've never read before. Buy the book if the first chapter holds your interest.
- Find a local park or running trail. Go for a walk or a jog.
- Google for "things to do in [your city]." Pick one.
- Volunteer for a day at a homeless shelter.

- Eat at a style of restaurant that you've never been to before—for instance, an ethnic restaurant or a vegan restaurant.

- Get some pencils and paper and try drawing something. Or buy some kids' art supplies and rediscover fingerpainting or coloring books.

- Visit a class for a type of exercise you've never done before.

- Drive to a nearby city that you've never been to before. Explore the city without looking up anything about it beforehand, and eat dinner at a local restaurant that you discover during your wanderings.

Quest Rewards:

- Build your confidence

- Expand your comfort zone

- Discover a new hobby or passion

Side Quests:

- Activate co-op mode! Invite a friend along to any of these experiences.

- Change something from your daily routine, and maintain that change for a whole week. For instance, if you normally switch on the computer immediately after waking up, see what happens if you read a book for ten minutes first. If you normally take the freeway home from work, see what happens if you take some side streets instead.

- Try something that you think you'll dislike, just to see what happens. For instance, even if you assume you dislike crowds, try going to a crowded concert. You might enjoy it more than you think—or you might learn that you can tolerate discomfort more than you thought.

Level Four
Go Into The Tall Grass

I'm a Pokémon purist.

I've only played Red and Blue and I think there are really only 150 Pokémon (151 if you count Missingno). Nowadays, when I listen to conversations about Pokémon, I'm flummoxed by everything that's new. There's IVs, EVs, new Pokémon types—and also Pokémon can be shiny now for some reason? An awful lot has changed.

But there's one constant since the first Pokémon game: if you want to find new Pokémon, you need to go into the tall grass.

Pokémon generally don't come to you. There's a specific place where you go if you want to catch them.

The same thing is true for meeting new potential friends. You need to go to the places where those connections are most likely to form.

Obviously, you can find people almost everywhere. But there are certain contexts where friendships are likely to grow, and contexts where they're not. While it's possible to befriend someone you meet in a grocery store, it's very unlikely. People don't come to grocery stores to socialize, so you're likely to come across as strange if you try to start a personal conversation.

Conversely, if you join something like a book club or a dance class, it's much easier to form friendships with the people you meet. At events like this, you have a lot of opportunities for conversation, and conversation is encouraged. Plus, you know you have at least one thing in common with everyone there.

It's easy to find the "tall grass" where potential friendships can be made. Just look for gatherings that fit these four criteria.

- This gathering should foster interaction between strangers. In other words, it should be easy for you to start a conversation with people that you do not know. A concert does not foster interaction, because most people going to a concert only talk with their friends. A theater class does foster interaction, because you will naturally interact with others as you practice your scenes together.

- The gathering should be something that you will probably enjoy doing. If you hate a particular activity, it will be hard to motivate yourself to go, and you will probably not get along super well with people who love that activity.

- The people at the gathering should be friendly, positive people. In other words, if you go to a social event and everyone seems rude and unfriendly, you might want to try another event.

- You should have the opportunity to meet new people every time you go. If you hang out with your best friends every Friday night, that's great, but it doesn't count for this quest because it doesn't give you the opportunity to meet new people.

To sum it up: If you want to expand your social circle, you need to go to events where you can meet new people that have the potential to be good friends. You need to go into the tall grass.

Quest 1.4 (Type: Weekly)

Quest Objectives:

- Go to a social gathering where you might meet new potential friends
- Do this once a week for one month.

Quest Description:

You can do the same gatherings each week or different ones—whichever option gives you the best chance of making friends. You can also try more than one social gathering each week if you like.

Some possible ways to find social gatherings:

- Check Meetup.com for groups that meet in your area
- Check the Craigslist activities and group sections (although use common sense and stay safe!)
- Contact the game stores in your area and see if they host any game nights.
- Google for [things to do] + [your city] or [places to meet people] + [your city]
- Research religious organizations in your area—most churches have community events throughout the week. If you're not religious, you might still make some friends at an event geared towards visitors.
- Look up classes for something that you're interested in—like theater, art, photography, or cooking.
- See if your community theater has open auditions
- Contact your local library and book stores and see if they have any book clubs.
- Check out Toastmasters.org and find a club near you (they're free to visit!)
- Look for volunteer opportunities.

- If you are a college student, look up clubs and student groups on campus, and visit one.

- Look for physical activities featuring social interaction—like a dance class or a team sport.

To sum it up: Once a week for a month, go somewhere fun where it's easy to meet new people. Sound like a plan?

Quest Rewards:

- Opportunity to meet new people

- Opportunity to practice your conversation skills

- Explore new hobbies and discover fun things to do.

Side Quests:

- Create a social gathering where other people can meet. The easiest way to do this is to plan an event where you invite different groups of friends. For instance, if you know people from a bowling league and from a theater class, organize a movie night where you invite both groups. That way people from the bowling league have the opportunity to befriend people from your theater class, and vice versa.

- Try for two or three events a week instead of one.

- Bring a friend to one of these events!

Level Five
Infinite Lives

In most classic games, you had a limited number of lives. Run out of lives, and it was game over—start back at the beginning. This design feature was inspired by arcade gaming, because it was in an arcade owner's best interest to force you to pony up more quarters for more lives.

But as arcades became less relevant for gaming, game developers started to reconsider the idea of limited lives. Why force a player to start over just because they used up their last life? So developers started phasing out the life system, and nowadays it's very rare to find a game that will show you a "Game Over" screen. In most modern games, dying just drops you back at your latest checkpoint, with no further consequence.

Of course, there are benefits to more high-stakes gameplay. In recent years rougelike games (where you get a single life and dying means starting from scratch) have become increasingly popular. When every decision counts, the game becomes much more engrossing.

But rougelikes can be exhausting to play. When a single mistake could mean that all of my progress is lost, I tend to anxiously ponder every decision. And when I do make a mistake, it can be deeply frustrating. I've yelled at my poor computer more than once when playing Don't Starve (and I still have unresolved anger towards those darn swamp tentacles.)

Of course, you bought a book on growing your social life, not a book on game design. So what's my point?

Simple.

In social settings, most people act like they're playing a rougelike. They assume that a single mistake will DOOM THEM FOREVER, so social interaction becomes about avoiding mistakes instead of having fun and connecting with others.

But here's the reality. In most social interactions, it's totally fine to make mistakes. In fact, everyone makes mistakes pretty much all the time in social interaction.

Don't believe me? Just listen in to everyone else next time you're in a group conversation. You'll hear the other people in the group interrupt each other, tell jokes that fall flat, share boring stories—all sorts of mistakes. And for the most part, everyone moves along with skipping a beat when those mistakes happen. Sure, maybe there's a moment of awkwardness, but then someone changes topics and the conversation moves along.

In other words, social interaction is more like a game with infinite lives than a rougelike game. Of course, it's better to avoid social mistakes if possible, and if you hurt or offended someone, you should definitely apologize and make amends.

But if you make a mistake, you get to try again. Even in a worst case scenario where you mess up a conversation so badly that the person doesn't want to talk to you anymore, you can always talk to someone else. There's always another social respawn waiting.

And that means you don't have to be afraid. You can let yourself relax, and maybe even be a little playful. If you make a mistake, it's okay— just apologize, and do your best to not repeat that mistake in the future.

Quest 1.5 (Type: Collection)

Quest Objectives:

- Make ten deliberate social mistakes
- See if the world ends

Quest Description

I promise, I'm not crazy.

Yes, I know you bought this book to find social success, not deliberately sabotage yourself. But hear me out.

If you're like many people, your fear of social failure is much bigger than it needs to be. When you spend so much time avoiding failure, you never get the chance to really enjoy social interaction. Who is going to have more fun—someone trying to make it through a game without losing a single life, or someone trying to explore all of the cool features the game designers programmed?

The cool thing about fear is that if you deliberately confront it, it tends to back down. The first time you ride a roller coaster, it's terrifying. The tenth time you ride it, it's probably not scary at all. That's what this quest is all about.

Of course, you should only do harmless mistakes. The goal is to choose social mistakes that feel scary, but that won't actually cause any harm to you or anyone else.

Here are some ideas:

- Deliberately tell a joke that isn't very funny. (Aka, Google for "dad jokes")
- Make plans with a friend. After making the plans, call back in an hour or so and ask to change some minor detail of the plans (for instance, ask if you can meet at 4 PM instead of 3 PM.)
- Leave your wallet in the car before entering a grocery store. Pick out something to buy, bring it to the register, then "real-

ize" that you forgot your wallet when it's time to pay. Apologize, get the wallet, and pay as normal.

You probably noticed that these ideas range from small mistakes (unfunny joke) to big mistakes (lost wallet.) When you try this yourself, I recommend starting with small mistakes, and working your way up to bigger and bigger mistakes. Just remember to never risk mistakes that could cause anyone real harm.

Also, if social interaction in general is very scary for you, I strongly encourage you to talk to a therapist. This level is designed to help people with moderate amounts of anxiety, but it's best to have a professional help you with high levels. The good news is that social anxiety is incredibly treatable. So talk with a therapist if your anxiety levels feel out of control or really distressing.

Quest Rewards:

- Less anxiety
- More confidence
- Fun stories to tell about your deliberate mistakes!

Side Quests:

- Read up on exposure therapy for social anxiety (that's where the ideas in this level are borrowed from.) Brainstorm a few new ideas for mistakes that you can practice making.
- If your level of anxiety feels higher than you'd like, research therapists in your area and consider contacting one.
- Before trying each social mistake, write down how you expect others will react. After doing the mistake, notice their reaction and compare it to your prediction.

Level Six
Hardware

I had hours of happy memories playing the original StarCraft during my childhood—I even set up a StarCraft LAN party for one of my birthdays. So it was a no-brainer that I would pick up StarCraft 2 soon after it was released.

Unfortunately, I quickly ran into a problem. My PC was full of aging components that I had not upgraded for years. My computer put up a valiant effort, but it just wasn't up to the challenge of rendering Star-Craft 2. See, as a game of StarCraft 2 progressed, the armies grew in size. This meant there were more units to render, which meant my poor computer had to work harder and harder, which meant that eventually it just couldn't keep up.

I would start a match with everything working fine. Then the map would start to fill with units, my computer would start to chug, and my frame rate would fall into the single digits. Needless to say, I did not win a lot of StarCraft 2 matches on my aging computer.

Fortunately, there was a solution to my problem. I patiently saved my money, and bought a bunch of shiny new PC parts. StarCraft 2 ran great on the new hardware, and I was able to win a lot more games.

You have hardware too—it's called your body. And just as my Star-Craft performance was impaired until I upgraded my computer, your social performance will be impaired if you don't take care of your body.

The reason is pretty simple. There's a ton of research that shows that if you exercise regularly, you'll have more energy and a happier mood. Now, let's say you're talking to someone. Are you more likely to make a positive impression if you're tired and sad, or if you're energetic and upbeat?

Of course, there are all sorts of other benefits to exercise that go beyond social interaction (like not dying from a heart attack.) But let's focus on the social benefits. If you take care of your body, your body will provide the power for you to put your best foot forward.

And you don't need to make dramatic changes to reap the benefit. The most important thing is to make a change that you can stick with. The CDC recommends 150 minutes of moderate exercise (ie, brisk walking, leisurely bicycling) or 75 minutes of vigorous exercise (ie, running, fast cycling) per week. That's not too bad—either 30 minutes of moderate exercise five times a week, or 25 minutes of vigorous exercise three times a week. You don't even need to do it all at once, so you could try getting in three ten-minute walking sessions instead of one thirty-minute walking session.

And if you're not exercising at all, you'll benefit from doing even half of what the CDC recommends. So try to start by doing just 15 minutes of walking five times a week, or going for a run just twice a week. Remember, the important thing is to pick something that you can stick with—so start slow and easy. If the very idea of exercise fills you with dread, start by walking for just ten minutes, three times a week. You can always build from there.

You can also try to make exercise more fun. For instance, you might join a class at the gym, or download an app like "Zombies Run." I personally like playing Hearthstone on my phone while using the cardio machines at the gym. I also love Dance Dance Revolution, because it's fun and a great workout. You can also try being active by doing things that don't feel like exercise, such as gardening. Experiment until you find something that works for you.

The important thing is to start and keep going. If you make a habit of exercise, you'll have more energy and a better mood, and that will pay big dividends when it comes time to be social. Plus, you might live longer, lose weight, and just generally be better off. The right exercise for you is the exercise you can stick with. So start exercising, and stick with it.

Oh, and one more thing. While exercise is very important, there are plenty of other ways that you can take care of your "hardware." Eating right, quitting smoking, sleeping 8 hours a night, getting regular checkups at the doctor—all of these things will help you out a lot. While the quest today will focus on exercise, here's a quick checklist for the other stuff:

- Are you are getting 8 hours of sleep per night? If not, Google for "sleep hygiene" and read up on tips to help you sleep better. You should also try going to bed earlier.

- Are you eating breakfast? If not, stop skipping breakfast. You'll gain more energy by taking ten minutes to eat breakfast than you would by getting ten more minutes of sleep.

- Do you have unhealthy habits you can't seem to stop (smoking, eating lots of junk food, etc)? If so, book an appointment with your doctor or a therapist. They should be able to help.

Quest 1.6 (Type: Monthly)

Quest Objectives:

- Exercise at least one hour a week
- Keep it up for at least a month
- (Optional) Exercise 2-3 hours per week.

Quest Description:

If you haven't exercised in a long time, you might just want to start with ten minutes of walking each day. If you feel like you're in pretty good shape, give yourself more of a challenge. The most important thing is to pick something you can stick with, which means picking something you don't hate. Start easy and get harder as you go along. (You can talk with your doctor or a trainer at the gym if you're not sure where a good place is for you to start.)

I recommend you do some research into the different types of exercise available. I used to hate exercise until I found out how to make it fun. Once I discovered sports like fencing or swing dancing, exercise became much more enjoyable for me. A friend of mine hated exercise until she discovered Couch to 5K and then she became really motivated to run. There are a ton of different ways to be active. Instead of starting with something you know you'll hate, look at your options and try to see if there is something that interests you.

Remember, your exercise doesn't need to feel like exercise to count. Go walking in a park or take the stairs instead of an elevator—every bit of extra movement adds up.

Your goal is consistency. If you stick with this for a month, you'll probably stick with it long term. Don't give up. So start small, start slow, but show up every time. Your hardware will stay healthy, you'll have more energy and a better mood, and the social payoff will be huge.

Quest Rewards:

- More energy

- Happier mood
- Better health

Side Quests:

- Exercise with a friend! Ask someone if they would be interested in exercising with you. For instance, you might find someone who would be a good running partner, or someone who would be willing to take an exercise class with you.

- Improve your diet! I don't recommend you try to dramatically overhaul your eating all at once (because you won't stick with it). But see if there is a single change you can make that will have a big impact. For instance, I stopped buying chips at the grocery store. When I had the chips in my house, I would always eat them. But if the chips never made it home with me, then I never really missed them (and my body certainly didn't miss the calories!). I also switched to diet soda and saved hundreds of calories each week. Start with simple changes like that, and build over time to improve your diet.

- Set yourself a fitness goal and work out a bit harder every week until you reach it. It's best if your goal is something that you can achieve in a month or two of good effort—after all, you can always give yourself a new goal.

Level Seven
It's Dangerous To Go Alone

In video games, the hero always seems to instantly adapt to the fact that their life has been turned upside down. Gordon Freeman is a nerdy scientist. Link is a dweeby kid. Mario fixes pipes for a living. None of them start their games as heroes or warriors.

Yet fifteen minutes into the game, they're killing enemies, dodging traps, and on a mission to save the world. And none of them seem fazed by this! It's like they've flipped a switch and effortlessly engaged hero mode.

Unfortunately, real life growth doesn't work that way. Real life change is often painful and slow. And real life change is hard to do alone. There's a reason why Weight Watchers and Alcoholics Anonymous are so popular—they've realized that if you try to change your life without any help, you're more likely to fail.

In other words, it really is dangerous to go alone.

By this point in the guide, you might be feeling a little of the pain that comes from making a life change. Being more social doesn't happen overnight—it requires unlearning old habits, building new skills, and being willing to challenge yourself. It might be tempting to think "I'll put this on pause for now"—and then never come back to it!

In other words, this is the point where you might benefit from a little support.

That's what today's quest is about.

Quest 1.7 (Type: Monthly)

Quest Objectives:

- Find someone you feel comfortable talking to about your social goals.
- Make a commitment to connect with them at least once a week for at least a month.

Quest Description:

It's up to you what your conversations with this person looks like. It could be as simple as you telling them how you are doing socially, and them giving you encouragement. Or you might have them help you plan social activities, or coach you on conversation skills. You could meet them in person, have a phone call, or even just share emails. Figure out what would be most helpful for you, and do that.

You have two options to find this person.

First, you can look for someone you already know—perhaps a trusted friend or family member. Make sure this is someone you can be honest with, someone who cares about you, and someone willing to help. You might even provide mutual support—for instance, maybe they can help encourage you socially, and you can encourage them with their fitness or academic goals.

If someone is immediately coming to mind as you read this, then you should probably talk to that person. If nobody is coming to mind, or if you feel awkward talking about your social growth with someone that you know, then this might not be the best option for you.

Your second option is to book a session with a professional therapist. Therapists are skilled at helping you achieve your goals, and they can also help you break through mental blocks or unconscious fears that hold you back from social connection. Especially if you are struggling emotionally (for instance, with depression or anxiety) a therapist is a great option.

While therapists do usually cost money to see, your health insurance might make therapy more affordable, and many therapists also offer "sliding scale" discounts for people struggling financially. Also, if you are a college student, most colleges offer free or low-cost counseling to students. So don't assume that money will be an obstacle.

Not sure how to find a therapist? A good place to start is usually by googling for "therapist in [my city]". You can also google for a therapist that focuses on your specific issue or group, for instance "anxiety therapist" or "therapist for teenagers." Look at a few of the websites that come up, and contact the therapist who seems like the best fit for you. Many therapists will offer a free phone consultation, so you can chat with them on the phone and see if you like them before you commit to a full session.

Whoever you pick, stick with it for at least a month. If you try someone and it doesn't work out, try someone else. I know it feels awkward to ask someone else for help—but trust me! Having someone in your corner makes it much more likely that you'll succeed.

Quest Rewards:

- Advice and encouragement
- Greater chance of social success
- Luke Skywalker had a mentor (Obi-Wan) so you will basically be like Luke which is super cool.

Side Quests

- Look for online support. A good place to start is Reddit.com/r/socialskills. /r/socialskills is an online community of 100,000 people that I moderate, and an excellent place to get advice and help as you become more social. You can also try 7 Cups of Tea (7Cups.com) which is a website where you can give and receive supportive listening.

- Look for an in-person group that will be supportive of you. Meetup.com sometimes has "introvert" or "social anxiety" meetups. While they might not fit your situation exactly, the people in those groups would probably support your desire to become more social.

- Try being your own support. Go to FutureMe.Org and write yourself some encouraging letters. You might want to set it up so that one arrives every week, or every month.

Stage Two: Multiplayer

Multiplayer Level One
Pong

When you ask people what the first video game was, most people will tell you "Pong!"

Most people are wrong.

Pong was actually pretty late to the party. In 1952, a computer version of Tic Tac Toe (called OXO) was developed, and Spacewar, the first shooter game, was developed in 1962. It wasn't until 1972—two decades after OXO—that Pong was released.

However, Pong is the game that is remembered. No doubt, this is mainly because of Pong's popularity. Pong was so successful that many people would visit their local bar just to play Pong, which is pretty impressive considering that Pong is just two lines and a glowing dot.

My introduction to Pong came decades later—not at a bar in the 70s, but on my TI-83 calculator in the 90s. See, the TI-83 calculator could run games, but only very basic ones. So old classics like Pong had a rebirth on my calculator, and I spent hours pinging that ball back and forth.

Around the time I discovered calculator Pong, I also started working on my social skills. And I noticed a lot of similarities between the skills required for Pong and the skills required for good conversation.

See, in a game of Pong, each player controls a paddle that travels up and down the screen. Players use their paddles to hit a ball back and forth, and score points when the other player fails to hit the ball.

Conversation resembles Pong in many ways, but with one crucial difference. In Pong, one person hits the ball, then the other person hits the ball, then it goes back to the first person who hits it again. In conversation, first one person speaks, and then the other person speaks, and then the first person speaks again. Instead of a ball, the conversation is the thing that moves back and forth between the two "players." So for instance,

You:

"Hey, good to see you! How was your weekend?"

It is now the other person's turn to speak, so you've sent the "ball" to them.

Them:

"Oh, nothing much, I mainly slept in and did some chores. Did you do anything fun?"

They've answered your question and asked you a question, so now it's your turn to speak—the ball is back on your side of the screen.

But here's the crucial difference. In Pong, you lose when you miss the ball, and you win when your opponent misses. But in conversation, you win when both of you hit the ball, and you lose if either of you miss.

Essentially, conversation is like a Pong game where the goal is to keep the volley going as long as possible. In order to "win" a conversation, you want to respond to what the other person says (returning the ball), and you want to make sure your response makes it easy for them to respond (aiming at their paddle so they can return the ball.)

Responding to what the other person said is pretty straightforward. If they ask a question, you want to answer it. If they make a statement, you want to acknowledge it in some way.

Making it easy for them to respond is a little more complicated but still pretty easy. Essentially, it means that you need to add something new to the discussion, and build on what they said. So perhaps you share an anecdote that relates to what they said, or you ask them a question, or you give them a few more details than they asked for.

Let's give an example.

Let's say someone says, "I hate this weather! It's so hot I can barely breathe." By saying this to you, they're trying to make a connection happen. To use the Pong metaphor, they're sending a ball your way. How do you respond?

A bad option would be if you ignore them. In that case, the ball sailed right past your paddle—not good.

A better option would be if you said "Yes, it's really hot!" In this case, you gave a response, so it's better than ignoring them. But you didn't make it easy for them to respond. They will probably struggle to think of something to say next, and the conversation will die out.

The best option would be if you said "Yes, it's really hot. I would love some ice cream!" Ok, this response won't win you any awards for eloquence. But it keeps the conversation going. You responded to them, and you offered up a new idea ("ice cream!") Now the other person can respond by talking about ice cream, or describing their favorite ways to keep cool.

Ok, I know I threw a lot at you. But it will make more sense as you practice it. And this is crucially important, because you can use this technique in almost all of your conversations. So to recap:

When it's your turn to talk in a conversation, make sure that you respond to what the other person said (hitting the ball), and add some new information or ask an interesting question so it's easy for them to respond to you (aiming the ball at their paddle so they can return it easily.) That 1-2 formula for talking in a conversation is a surefire way to make your conversations flow more smoothly. And who knows? Maybe it will give you a new appreciation for Pong, too.

Oh, and one final note: Once you master this technique, you can also use it to gauge whether or not other people are interested in talking with you. If the other person is "playing Pong" by responding to your comments and adding new information, you can be pretty confident that they want to talk to you. But if the other person keeps missing the balls you're sending their way, probably they just want to be left alone and you should find someone else to talk to.

Quest 2.1 (Type: Collection)

Quest Objectives:

- Play "Conversational Pong" for ten conversations. Instructions:

- In each conversation, do your best to respond to what the other person said (hitting the ball)

- Also, do your best to add new information or ask a good question in every response (aiming the ball at the paddle).

- (Optional) Keep track of how long you can keep a conversational volley going. Try to beat your high score!

Quest Description:

The easiest way to practice conversational pong is in chat rooms. Real-world conversation requires fast responses and online chat gives you more opportunity to think through what you're going to say (which is great for practice.) Of course, if you prefer to practice in your real-life conversations, that's fine too.

If you need a chat room to practice in, I recommend you head to the /r/socialskills IRC chatroom (located at https://kiwiirc.com/client/ irc.snoonet.org/socialskills/). Ask if anyone would like to do conversation practice with you. Spend at least ten minutes chatting, and practice your "conversational pong" skills. At the end of the conversation, ask your partner for honest feedback.

Warning: Don't force someone to stay in a conversation forever. If the other person doesn't seem interested in continuing the conversation, it's okay to stop playing conversational pong with them and let the conversation die. It's better to have a short conversation that feels great than a lengthy conversation that drags on far too long.

Quest Rewards:

- Smooth, flowing conversations
- More confidence in conversation

- Others will enjoy talking to you more.

Side Quests:

- Head to PongGame.org and play a few games of Pong. Not only is it a piece of gaming history, but it will give you a good visual image to use when you are in a conversation.

- Watch a TV show that has a lot of dialogue (reality TV shows can be great for this). Pick a character. Whenever someone says something to that character, pause the show and imagine that you are that character. Take a moment to think how you would respond in a way that returns the ball and aims at their paddle. Then unpause and see how the character actually responded.

- Check out my full conversation guide at ImproveYourSocial-Skills.com/Conversation. It's free, and it goes much more in depth.

Multiplayer Level Two
Minecraft

Ok, I'll confess.

I've only played Minecraft once. My college roommate played it fanatically, and one day I asked to try it. I punched a few trees, chased a few pigs, built a pickaxe, mined straight down, and found myself trapped once my pickaxe broke. I logged off and have not returned.

But I've enjoyed sinking my teeth into similar games. My favorite is Terraria, with well over a hundred hours played. Being 2D, Terraria doesn't have quite the building potential as Minecraft, but it makes up for it with excellent co-op and a good blend of exploration, mining, combat, and crafting. Given how much fun I've had with Terraria, one of these days I might finally bite the bullet and return to the original land of pickaxes and pig punching (this time, I'll dig stairs instead of an inescapable pit!)

There's something extremely compelling about games like Minecraft or Terraria, where the same raw materials can turn into everything from a sturdy creeper defense to an intricate recreation of Middle Earth. Obviously, a game as popular as Minecraft has a lot of enjoyable features. But for the purposes of this book, I want to highlight just one—gathering resources for crafting.

See, here's the thing. When you play Minecraft or Terraria, you come across a lot of resources during your exploring. On occasion you're hunting for a particular resource because you have a goal in mind, but often you don't know exactly what you'll need down the road. So a savvy player will gather a variety of valuable resources during their explorations, so later on they have a stockpile of resources ready for any crafting project.

Here's where I'm going with this. Conversation is kind of like crafting, in that good conversation requires some "raw resources." In this case, raw resources are things like interesting stories from your life, hot topics in the news, or knowledge about what's happening in the life of the person you're talking with. If you never know what to say in a conversation, you may need to do more "mining" beforehand.

For instance, as I write this in early 2016, the big news is Donald Trump running for president. Most people like talking about The Donald's latest antics, so knowledge about him is a valuable resource. If you know the recent news about Donald Trump, you can start a conversation by saying, "So, what do you think about Donald Trump running for president?" or "Hey, did you heard that Donald Trump did X recently?" In this case, the resource that you mined was the latest news on Donald Trump, and you were able to craft that news into a good conversation topic.

There are lots of ways you can mine conversational resources. One good way is to keep up to date on the news and discussion surrounding popular hobbies. One of my friends started a job at a new office where everyone loved sports. My friend didn't like sports, but he did want to connect with his new coworkers. So he started watching *Sports Center* and after about a month, he could participate in conversations about sports without missing a beat.

You can do the same thing. Find a good website, podcast or TV show that discusses the topic you want to be more knowledgeable about, and after a few weeks you'll be able to participate in conversations on that topic. For instance, if you wanted to stay up to date on gaming news, visit Kotaku a few times a week. If you want to stay up to date on world news, visit The New York Times or the Economist.

There's really a good source of news for almost any hobby you can think of. I don't know anything about fishing, but a few seconds on Google revealed that WorldFishingNetwork.com exists. If I had a friend who loved fishing, that would be a great site to add to my weekly routine. After I read World Fishing Network for a few weeks, I would have good questions that I could ask my friend about their favorite hobby. You can do this too. Just Google for the name of their hobby, plus "news" or "blog."

Another excellent way to mine for conversational resources is to stay alert for interesting stories in your own life. If something interesting, exciting or unusual happens to you, make an effort to remember it (you might even write it down.) You may find that it becomes a great story to share during conversations.

For instance, I went on a terrible date in college, which was not at all fun at the time (I won't go into detail, but it ended when her friend called midway through the date, and she canceled the date to hang out with her friend instead.) But later on, I realized how funny the story of my terrible date was, and I've since told that story in dozens of conversations and received lots of laughs. So keep alert for the interesting or unusual things that happen in your life, and see if they might become stories that you can add to conversation.

Of course, you can also try to deliberately have some interesting experiences in order to build your stockpile of stories. I once got an opportunity to ride along as a retired professional racer drove on a Formula One race track. It was terrifying, but it made for a great story. You could try bungee jumping, or enter a pie eating contest, or volunteer at an old folks' home. Do something out of the ordinary, and over time you'll build a lot of stories you can use in conversations.

One final source of resources: Your conversation partners themselves. Often when you're talking with someone, they'll tell you facts that you can use in later conversations. For instance, if a friend tells that they're about to embark on a big road trip, remember that fact. Then next time you talk to them, ask them how the road trip went. You'll score points for your good memory, and you'll start a good conversation.

(Warning: Avoid the temptation to snoop. Information that someone tells you directly is fair game, but if you have to troll through their Facebook to find information, you may want to think twice before bringing it up, especially if you don't know them well.)

Quest 2.2 (Type: Daily)

Quest Objectives:

- Choose two to three good sources you can mine for conversational resources
- Check each source each day for a week.

Quest Description:

During lunch I often check Google News for general news, ArsTechnica.com for technology news, and Reddit to stay up-to-date on the internet hive mind. But you don't need to be limited to websites. If you spend a lot of time in the car, try downloading some good podcasts, or tune into an informative station like NPR. You might even subscribe to a print magazine (they still exist!)

Please note: these need to be sources of news that discuss different topics. If you pick three different sources of gaming news, all you can discuss is gaming. So find news sources that address a variety of topics.

At first, pick news sources that you're really going to enjoy reading, to make the habit stick. But as you progress, you might want to add news sources that relate to a topic that would be good for you to learn. For instance, you might follow news for the industry you work in. Or you might follow news related to a friend's hobby. You might even decide to teach yourself a particular skill, and start following the latest tips on personal finance or exercise (or even social skills!)

Whatever you choose, be consistent about it. Ten or fifteen minutes per day is plenty, but ten or fifteen minutes per month is not. Find a way to make this part of your routine, and stick with it.

Quest Rewards:

- More topics you can use in conversation
- Be more informed and educated
- Discover new areas of interest.

Side Quests:

- Do something interesting, just for the story. Try speed dating! Go to the zoo and feed the llamas! Take an art class! Wake up early and hike to a hilltop, then watch the sunrise. If it would make a good story, give it a try!

- Spend one week following the news on a topic that you're not familiar with, and see what you can learn.

- When your friend tells you something about their life, remember it and bring it up in a future conversation.

Multiplayer Level Three
Parsers

My favorite childhood games, without a doubt, were the King's Quest series. The King's Quest series were classic adventure games—you traveled throughout a fantasy kingdom, collecting items, solving puzzles, and generally being heroic. As a kid, these games were perfect for imagining myself as the hero on a quest, and I would play them constantly.

Of course, some of the reason I put so many hours into them was that my progress was slow. While later King's Quest games moved to a point-and-click interface, the early ones used a parser interface. In a parser interface, you type in the actions you wanted your character to perform.

For instance, if your character fell in a lake, you would type SWIM. If you wanted your character to climb a tree, you would type CLIMB TREE. You could move around the world with the arrow keys, and you could get some information by looking at the graphics, but mostly you interacted with the game by typing commands. As a kid, this was a challenging interface to master, because my vocabulary and spelling were both limited—making it difficult for me to figure out exactly what I needed to type in to the parser to solve a particular puzzle.

However, I eventually learned an excellent strategy for using the parser. If you use the LOOK command, the game will print a description of the area you're in, including all of the different objects in the area. I could then use the game's words for the objects in order to interact with them.

For instance, at one point in King's Quest 2, you encounter what looks like a pitchfork lying on the beach. But typing GET PITCH-FORK returned an error message. It was only when I first used LOOK that I realized the object on the beach was a trident—and then successfully grabbed it using GET TRIDENT.

In other words, I didn't need to rely on my own (limited) vocabulary anymore. I could LOOK and then use the game's words from the description to guide my action.

While I didn't realize it at the time, I think this realization also helped me in my conversations.

See, here's the thing. When you talk to someone, you need to have something to talk about. But if you pick a boring topic (or no topic at all), the conversation will quickly peter out. So how do you know what to talk about?

People try to solve this problem in different ways. Some people have a stockpile of interesting questions ready, and jump from one prepared question to the next. Some people wait for the other person to take the initiative and ask them a question. Other people just start talking about whatever they want, and hope the other person shares their interest.

But there's a better option. Just give your partner the opportunity to show you what they want to talk about.

See, people will signal to you the topics they want to discuss. You just need to give them a chance. If you give people an open-ended question, they will usually answer it in a way that suggests the topics they want to discuss.

For instance, let's say you ask someone, "Hey, what's new?" and they respond "Oh, I just got a new dog, so I've been busy taking care of him." They could have answered your question any way they wanted to. Because they chose to mention the dog, there's a pretty good chance that they would welcome a conversation about their new dog.

Or to put it back in King's Quest terms—by asking an open ended question, you were essentially typing LOOK. Your follow up question should be based on the reply, just as the follow up actions in the game are based on what LOOK tells you about the environment.

Here's a detailed example. In King's Quest you might type "LOOK" and receive the reply "You stand in a wooden glade. A large boulder rests beneath the shade of the trees." The boulder is the most interesting part of the description, so you type "LOOK BOULDER" and receive the reply "The boulder is weathered and grey, with a large hole in the side. Something glints from inside the hole." The hole is the most interesting part of the boulder, so you type "LOOK HOLE" and the game tells you "A beautiful diamond necklace lies abandoned within the hole." Finally, you type "GET NECKLACE" and are rewarded with a valuable item.

In a conversation, you might say "What's new?" which leads to "Oh, I just got a new dog." The dog is the most interesting part of the answer, so you ask a question like "Wow, a dog! What's it like to be a dog owner?" Your question remains open-ended, but you are showing interest. Your partner might respond, "I love it! I think my favorite part is when we get to go to the park and play together." The most interesting part of the answer is playing at the park, so you ask, "Aw, that sounds fun. What do you guys do together at the park?"

Just as LOOK leads to LOOK BOULDER which leads to LOOK HOLE which leads to GET NECKLACE, "What's new?" leads to "What's it like to be a dog owner?" which leads to "What do you do at the dog park?" In both cases, the progression is natural and intuitive. All you need to do is ask an open-ended question, look for the key ideas that you get from the response, and then ask another open-ended question that builds on those key ideas.

Of course, you can run into some wrinkles along the way. For instance, what if they include multiple key ideas in their response? In that case, pick the one that interests you the most. It's easier to ask good questions if you have genuine curiosity.

You can also go back to key ideas that were mentioned earlier. For instance, if someone says "This weekend I'm going to the mall and then I'm going on a road trip" you could ask them about the mall and then ask them about the road after you're finished discussing the mall. This backtracking is especially helpful if you choose the wrong key topic to ask about. If you ask them about the mall and they seem bored with your question, you might switch immediately to asking about the road trip.

By the way, you don't need to stick with one topic for this technique to work. For instance, midway through a conversation about their new dog, someone might say "I'm really excited for when he's old enough to take to the office with me." They've just introduced a new key idea—the office—and so you can now ask them questions about their job if you like.

Quest 2.3 (Type: Collection)

Quest Objectives

- LOOK (ask an open-ended question) in conversation ten times
- FOLLOW UP (ask about the key idea from their response) ten times.

Quest Description

Pretty straightforward. Ask someone an open ended question, and then ask them a follow up question based on their answer. You should do this ten times total, but you don't need to do all ten in the same conversation.

At first, you might struggle a little. It can be difficult to come up with open-ended questions on the fly, and it can also be difficult to tell which part of their answer you should respond to. But with practice, you'll build a collection of good open-ended questions, and you'll also get better at sensing which part of their response is really the most important. Remember, you don't need to be perfect at this— just keep practicing, and you'll get better over time.

Quest Reward:

- +2 to asking questions
- +4 to conversational skill
- +9 against ogres

Side Quests:

- Play King's Quest! Okay, this one won't help you much with your social skills. But it will help you understand the parser reference, and it's just a fun game in general. You can play the original King's Quest games for free at Sarien.net, or you can download a more modern fan remake at AGDInteractive.com. They're also for sale on Steam and Gog.com. The modern remakes don't use the parser, but you can still get a feel for the gameplay.

- Practice adding topic suggestions when you reply to other people's questions. For instance, I usually add one or two details to any response that I offer so the other person has something to ask about. Instead of saying "My weekend was good" I might say "My weekend was good. I had lunch with a friend, and then we saw a new movie together!" That way they can ask me about the friend, or the movie if they want.

- Next time you read a novel, pause whenever two characters have a detailed conversation. Challenge yourself to identify the key topics in their responses, and practice the questions you would ask if you were present. Of course, this won't work with every book or with all dialog. But this is a good way to practice on your own.

Multiplayer Level Four
The Whelk

Final Fantasy Six (originally released as Final Fantasy Three in the US) was a masterpiece of a game. Despite being constrained by the technical limitations of the SNES, it managed to fit deep characters, engrossing plot, a sweeping orchestral score, and fantastic gameplay into a 16 bit cartridge.

If you've never played it, you are missing out. There is a reason why this game is still regularly featured on "best game of all time" lists, even more than twenty years after it was originally released. Fortunately, you can buy a remade version on Android or iPhone (and I highly recommend you do!)

However, I'm not going to talk about what made FF6 great. I'm not going to talk about the story, the characters, the gorgeous opera scene, or the dancing Moogles.

Instead, I'm going to talk about the first boss you face in that game—the Whelk.

The Whelk is basically a giant magical snail. Kind of weird, I know, but it's not exactly the weirdest enemy that's ever appeared in a Final Fantasy game.

Anyway, the Whelk is the first boss you face in the game. He's also the first puzzle. See, you can target either the Whelk's head or his shell. If you target the head, you deal good damage. If you target his shell, he blasts your party with a high-damage lightning bolt.

But the Whelk has a trick. It will periodically pull its head inside its shell. If he pulls his head inside the shell, you need to hold your fire until the head reemerges or risk getting zapped to oblivion.

In other words, your fight with the Whelk quickly becomes a red light/green light kind of situation. When the Whelk's head is poking out, you have a green light—time to attack. When his head is hidden in the shell, you have a red light—hold your fire!

At first, the Whelk seems like a formidable foe. But as soon as you figure out the pattern, it goes down easily.

The same thing is true of body language. Interpreting body language can seem like a daunting task. But as soon as you learn the red light/green light pattern that body language follows, it becomes easy to understand.

See, here's the thing. There are tons of body language guides out there that claim to explain the meaning of every eyebrow wiggle and nose scratch. And while many of those guides are written by expert authors who know what they're talking about, the simple fact is that it's almost impossible for the average person to memorize hundreds of body language signals—let alone learn how to recognize and interpret them in a real conversation.

Yet, body language is critical for social success. By successfully reading body language, you are better able to tell what other people are thinking, better able to decide on the best way to interact with them, and better able to gauge how well you are performing socially. So you need some way to read body language in conversation.

The solution? Red light/green light (or if you prefer, "whelk shell" or "whelk head.") Your goal is not to figure out every single nuance of body language. Instead, you just need to figure out if they other person is feeling mostly comfortable, or if they are feeling mostly uncomfortable. Again, it's not important to figure out exactly what they're feeling. You just need to know if there's a problem, or if everything is okay.

In other words, you don't need to learn how to recognize all of the individual meanings of each body language signal. Instead, you can just ask yourself, "Is this usually a good signal, or usually a bad signal?"

If the other person is giving off lots of signals that are usually bad, you can assume something is probably wrong and try to fix it (red light/whelk shell). If the other person is giving off lots of signals that are usually good, you can assume everything is probably okay, and then relax (green light/whelk head.)

As an example, let's say you're talking to a friend and your dog enters the room. If your friend starts to exhibit positive body language signals, you can assume they like dogs and everything is fine. If your friend's body language doesn't change, you can assume they don't really care about dogs (and again, everything is fine.) If your friend's body language becomes negative, it's possible your friend is afraid of dogs or allergic to them. In that case, you should probably ask,

"Would you like me to put the dog outside?" or take some other action to solve the problem.

Or imagine you ask your friend a personal question. If their body language is positive or neutral, you can assume that they don't mind your question. But if their body language immediately becomes negative, you can assume they probably don't want to answer such a personal question. Then you can use that assumption to guide your behavior as you immediately try to comfort them—for instance, by saying "I'm sorry, that was a really personal question. Please don't answer if you feel uncomfortable."

Of course, all of this begs the question "How do you recognize if body language is positive or negative?"

Well, the best way is to spend time with the body language books I mentioned earlier. But instead of trying to memorize the exact meaning of each body language signal, just try to remember if it is generally a good signal (communicating happiness and comfort) or a bad signal (communicating stress and unhappiness.) This will make it much easier to memorize.

If you don't have the time to dive into the body language books, here's two tips to get you started:

First, tension versus relaxation. A comfortable person will look relaxed – they will be sitting or standing in a comfortable way, they won't demonstrate a lot of nervous energy, and their voice will be calm. An uncomfortable person will look tense and stressed—they might be pacing nervously, or rubbing their face, or demonstrating some tension in their voice.

Second, closeness versus distance. If a person feels comfortable with you, they will move to close the distance between you. They might walk closer to you, or they might turn to face you, or they might lean in if you are both sitting down. Conversely, a person who is uncomfortable will add distance by leaning back, turning away, or moving further away.

In other words, if a person is relaxed, facing you directly, and not too far away, you probably have a green light. If a person is tense, turning away from you or otherwise putting distance between the two of you, there might be a problem—and you should try to fix it.

Of course, body language is complex, and the meaning of body language can vary based on the situation. For instance, a person might appear tense when they talk to someone they are attracted to—so tension in that context wouldn't be a bad thing at all. Or someone might move closer to someone else when arguing with them—which is a sign of hostility, not comfort. But these big ideas (tension vs relaxation, closeness vs distance) work pretty well as a rule of thumb for gauging if someone is comfortable or not. And as you continue to practice and study, you'll get better and better at judging body language.

If you want some more specific tips, you can check out my free guide at ImproveYourSocialSkills.com/Body-Language. I also strongly recommend Joe Navarro's book *What Every BODY Is Saying*. The good news is that you can start using the red light/green light technique right away, even without extra advice.

So to sum up: In order to read body language, just try to figure out if someone is mostly comfortable or mostly uncomfortable. If they're comfortable, then great! If they're uncomfortable, see if there is something you can do to fix it. To figure out if they're comfortable or uncomfortable, gauge their level of relaxation, and gauge whether they're moving closer to you or further away.

Quest 2.4 (Type: Daily)

Quest Objectives:

- Watch a movie or TV show with the volume on mute. Youtube clips of people having conversations will also work.

- As you watch, guess if the people you're watching are comfortable or uncomfortable, based on their body language. Then rewind and watch again with the volume on so you can see if your guess was correct.

- Do this once a day for a week.

Quest Description:

Make sure you pick a show where there is lots of conversation and emotion—reality TV shows might be good for this. 15 minutes per day or so is probably plenty. You're not learning how to read every single piece of body language; you're just getting a general sense of whether or not there's a problem.

Quest Rewards:

- Pick up on people's reactions to the things you say and do

- Notice problems quickly

- Be kind of like a mind reader.

Side Quests:

- Grab a book of body language signals (like "What Every BODY Is Saying.") Flip through it and pick a handful of body language signals to memorize—being careful to memorize them as just "comfort" or "discomfort" instead of trying to remember exactly what they mean. (It's okay to memorize exact meanings later if you want.) Then, try to recognize those specific signals next time you watch TV or a movie.

- Go to a mall food court or somewhere else where you can unobtrusively observe others interacting. Watch the people around you as they converse, and guess whether they are comfortable or uncomfortable based on their body language. Make sure you're not staring!

- Start to notice your own body language. Remember, your body language sends signals as well. So if you are demonstrating uncomfortable body language, you're telling other people "something is wrong" or "stay away." If those aren't the signals you mean to send, try relaxing and giving more positive body language signals, and see what happens!

Multiplayer Level Five
PVP

World of Warcraft is a game built around violence.

It's possible to spend many hours roleplaying in Goldshire or trading at the auction house, but when it comes right down to it, most people spend their time in WoW murdering monsters and battling other players in PVP.

After all, that's the only way to proceed, right?

Well, not if you're Noor the pacifist. Noor (named after Noor Inayat Khan, a pacifist who aided the French Resistance against the Nazis) was the first WoW character who made it all the way to max level without killing a single other character. While others have come after him, Noor was the first to accomplish this feat—and he did it earlier in WoW's history, when it was much harder to level without combat.

Noor showed that it was possible to be peaceful in a game where everyone else was being violent. Easy, no. But possible, yes (and rewarding, too!) After all, in a game with 100 million other players, Noor is one of the few who have become famous.

Noor's story shows an important truth about handling social conflict. When conflict starts, people often move immediately to a me-vs-you or us-vs-them mentality. The assumption is that the only way forward is to win while the other person loses.

When this happens, people start treating each other like enemies. Instead of calmly discussing the problem, they yell over each other. Instead of focusing on the issue at hand, they bring up past arguments, or make personal attacks. Usually when things devolve to this level, the problem never really gets solved—one person gives in to stop the fighting, but remains upset.

But there's another way. You can choose the pacifist path when it comes to conflict. Instead of treating the other person like an enemy that you need to defeat, you can treat them the way that you'd want to be treated – with respect and kindness. You can avoid hurtful comments, and try to phrase your complaints in a respectful way. You can listen patiently to the other person's position, and wait to disagree until you're sure that you completely understand it. Most of all, you can work towards a mutually beneficial solution—where both of you win and nobody loses.

Being a pacifist is not the same as being passive. You don't need to bottle up your feelings or agree with someone else when they say hurtful things about you. But you do need to stand up for yourself in a way that is calm and respectful, and you need to seek the good of everyone, not just yourself.

This "Noor the Pacifist" approach to interpersonal conflict is difficult to do. When you are upset or offended, it's easy to lash out. And even if you do your best to try to resolve a conflict amicably, the other person might resist your efforts. So resolving conflicts peacefully is hard to do, and it doesn't always work.

But when it does work, it's awesome. You can save friendships, you can dispel negative feelings, and you can get a reputation as a peacemaker. Plus, it gets easier with practice—and getting you practice is what this quest is all about.

Quest 2.5 (Type: Collection)

Quest Objectives:

- When in an argument, calmly work towards a solution where everyone feels satisfied.

- Do this in three separate arguments.

- If you end up losing your temper in an argument or failing to work towards a solution, sit down after the dust has settled and think through what happened. Make a plan for getting a better outcome next time.

Quest Description:

The next time you get into an argument, calmly work towards a solution where everyone feels satisfied.

Ok, I know. This is much easier said than done. But here are a few tips to get you started:

- Avoid personal attacks and name-callings. Focus on the problem, not attacking the other person. For example, if you are upset with someone for always arriving late, say something like "It really messes with our plans when you arrive late" rather than "You are so lazy and rude!

- Make sure you understand what the other person is saying before you respond. I recommend that you wait until they finish speaking (don't interrupt), and then try to summarize their argument before you offer your own thoughts. If you don't understand where they're coming from, it's impossible to figure out a solution that works for both of you.

- Remember that the best solution is probably a compromise. Be creative and try to see if there are any ways that both people can get what they want.

These ideas are only a start. If you really want to improve your conflict resolution skills, I encourage you to read the book *Crucial Conversations*. You could also think about seeking therapy to help build your conflict resolution skills. Keep in mind though that this strategy only works if the other person is open to compromise—if they are just trying to antagonize you, then you should use the "turtling" strategy we cover in the next level.

Remember that you don't need to be an expert to have good conflict resolution skills. The biggest difference is in your mindset. If you go into an argument determined to win, you will probably hurt the other person and cause them to resent you. If you go into an argument determined to restore peace and solve the problem in a way that works for everyone, you will probably end up at a great resolution.

This won't be easy. But even if it doesn't work, you'll be glad you tried. So give it a shot!

Quest Rewards:

- Resolve arguments peacefully
- Avoid long conflicts and hard feelings
- Don't lose friendships over silly fights.

Side Quests:

- Spend a few minutes thinking about the people you've hurt recently. If some names come to mind, give them a call or email and apologize. Even though they might have hurt you as well, take the high road and end the conflict.

- Build your skill in handling conflicts. As I've mentioned, the best book for this is *Crucial Conversations*—it's an easy read, and you'll feel more confident even after the first few chapters.

- If it's very easy for you to become angry and "fly off the handle", consider seeing a professional therapist. A good therapist can really help you manage your anger.

Multiplayer Level Six
Turtling

When I was in middle school, I discovered the original *StarCraft* and was immediately blown away. I didn't particularly care about the strategic complexity of the game or the rich story—remember, I was in middle school!

Instead, I loved demolishing the computer. It felt great to build row after row of bunkers or proton cannons, and let the stupid AI waste its units rushing into my defenses. The strategy I used is called "turtling", after a turtle hunkering down in its shell. As a kid though, I just called it "Mwahahaha!"

Of course, turtling is not as effective against human opponents. When you're dependent on a row of fixed defenses, a clever opponent can easily go around, or destroy your defenses from long range. But as a kid playing against the computer, turtling made me invincible.

And as an adult, I found a social technique that protected me against harassment—which I also called turtling.

Here's how it works.

Let's say someone is trying to harass you. Maybe you've done something to irritate them, maybe they're a bully, or maybe they're just bored. But for whatever reason, they're attempting to tease you, or perhaps they're trying to pressure you into talking about a sensitive topic that you'd rather keep private.

That's when you turtle.

Turtling, in this context, means that you stay calm and polite, and you give them the exact same answer every time until they go away.

For instance:

Them:
"Hey, I heard that your girlfriend broke up with you. What happened—did she find someone better?

You:
"You know, that's really none of your business."

Them:
> "C'mon, I just want to know the story. What's the big deal? Just tell me what happened."

You:
> "You know, that's really none of your business."

Them:
> "Seriously dude? Stop being so uptight. Just tell me what happened."

You:
> "You know, that's really none of your business."

Them:
> "Ok, whatever." [Leaves]

See how this works? You stayed polite and calm, and you also stayed firm. You repeated the same phrase over and over, and this made it clear that you weren't going to talk about the breakup. Eventually, they realized you weren't going to budge, and they wandered off. This is turtling in a nutshell.

The key to turtling is to give them the same response every single time. Remember, generally when people are harassing you, they are looking for some kind of reaction. If they can see you getting emotional, or if you start giving them interesting answers, then they will keep harassing you. But if you give them the same response every single time, then you will quickly become boring to them and they'll leave you alone. This works best if you keep your voice calm, but it will still work even if your tone betrays some stress. The important thing is to clearly show the other person that you won't budge.

Turtling also works with friends. If your friend is being obnoxious, you don't want to get angry with them. But if you turtle, you can often signal to them that they should quiet down.

For instance,

Friend:
> "Hey, whatcha doing?"

You:
> "I'm trying to finish this project—it's almost due and I'm running out of time."

Friend: [Not getting the hint]
>"Oh, that's cool. I'm just hanging out. Anyway, what are you doing this weekend?"

You:
>"Right now, I'm just trying to finish this project that's almost due"

Friend: [Still not getting the hint]
>"Aw, that's boring. Why don't you tell me about the weekend instead?"

You:
>"Right now, I'm just trying to finish this project that's almost due"

Friend: [Finally getting the hint]
>"Oh, okay. I'll leave you alone so you can focus."

(Of course, you could also just tell your friend "Hey, I can't talk right now." But if they don't get the hint, then you can just turtle and that will quickly drive your point home, without being offensive.)

Unfortunately, turtling only works against verbal harassment. If someone is threatening you with violence, that's your cue to leave. But since verbal harassment is much more common than physical aggression, turtling is an excellent skill to have.

Quest 2.6 (Type: Collection)

Quest Objectives:

- Practice turtling five times

Quest Description:

The easiest way to practice turtling is if you have a friend or family member who can help you. Just ask someone to pretend to tease you, then respond to their teasing with turtling. If you end up getting flustered and forgetting to turtle, reset and try again. Keep practicing until you can maintain your turtle phrase without a problem. Success means that you were able to calmly repeat your turtle phrase until the other person got bored and ran out of things to say.

If you don't have another person who can help you, it's still possible to practice. Just place two chairs facing each other. Make one chair the "teasing" chair and one chair the "turtle" chair. Start by sitting in the "teasing" chair, and try to tease yourself. Then move to the "turtle" chair and try to respond by turtling. It will feel a little goofy to move between the chairs (and I don't recommend doing this in public!) but this will help you get into character. Pretty soon, it should feel pretty natural, and then you can practice against yourself. Think of it like single-player chess.

Quest Rewards:

- The ability to stay calm when someone is teasing you
- Avoid telling people personal information you don't want to share.
- Make it harder for others to bother you

Side Quests:

- Brainstorm some "turtle phrases" (such as "I'm sorry, I'm not interested" or "I'm sorry, but I'm not going to talk about that") that you can memorize and use when necessary

- Play a game of StarCraft (or another RTS) against the computer. Experiment with a turtling defense.

- Keep your eyes open for other people who engage in "turtling." If someone starts to turtle in response to your questions, that's a sign that you should change the topic and stop pestering them.

Multiplayer Level Seven
Sandbox Gameplay

Sandbox games are phenomenally fun.

In sandbox games like Minecraft, Skyrim or Grand Theft Auto, the developers don't force you to follow a set storyline or pursue specific objectives. Instead, the game hands you a massive world to explore, a ton of fun things to do, and lets you do whatever you want.

I think part of why sandbox games are so popular is because they are deeply immersive. Your ability to create whatever kind of experience you like allows you to play the game in a way that feels right to you. Skyrim allows you to be a selfless hero, a greedy thief—or a tourist who just wants to wander around and admire the scenery. Minecraft allows you to be an explorer, a builder, or just a pig puncher. You have the freedom to add your own personality to the gameplay experience, and that's why so many people love them. Other games that put you on a rigid pathway might have beautiful graphics and fun gameplay, but they don't suck you in quite the way a sandbox does.

As you might have guessed, there's a connection to social skills here. See, when you talk to someone, you can make the experience like a sandbox, or like a traditional linear game. You can either give someone the freedom to build something that shows their own personality, or you can drag them along a rigid path. While the rigid pathway can be easier to create, giving someone a "sandbox" conversation is more likely to create connection.

So how do you create a sandbox conversation?

Well, you need to follow two steps.

First, ask open-ended questions instead of closed ended questions. Closed-ended questions can only be answered in a few ways, while open-ended questions can be answered however the person likes. For instance, if you ask someone "How many siblings do you have?" they can only really answer by giving a number. However, if you ask someone "What is your family like?" they can answer however they want.

Second, ask questions with subjective answers, not objective answers. In other words, ask questions about experiences and emotions, not facts. Subjective questions invite the other person to talk about what it's like to be them. They invite the other person to share their feelings, their memories, their unique experiences. Conversely, questions with objective answers tend to stifle connection. Asking someone "What were you like as a child?" is more likely to spark a good conversation than asking "Where did you grow up?"

Obviously, there is a lot of overlap between these two steps. Subjective questions are much more likely to be open-ended than objective questions. But there are some subjective closed ended questions ("What is your favorite memory from childhood?") and some objective open ended questions ("What did you do this weekend?") If possible, ask questions that are both open ended and subjective. If you can't do that, at least try to ask questions that are at least one or the other.

Note that it's okay to ask closed-ended objective questions sometimes. There's nothing wrong with asking someone what they do for a living, or how old they are. But closed-ended objective questions do not tend to lead to deeper connections or great conversations, so you should make an effort to use open-ended, subjective questions when possible.

As a metaphor, even sandbox games have some linear gameplay elements (Skyrim starts with a linear tutorial, for instance.) But a good sandbox game developer tries to give the player as much freedom as possible. As a good conversationalist, you should do the same.

Quest 2.7 (Type: Daily)

Quest Objectives:

- Ask at least one "sandbox" (open ended and subjective) question per day.
- Do this for one week.

Quest Description:

I'm starting you small on this quest—only one question per day.

But there's a reason I structured it this way. I want asking sandbox questions to become a habit for you, and the easiest way to accomplish that is through consistency. So it's better for you to ask one question each day than for you to ask a million questions on day one and then forget about it on day two.

Of course, you are welcome to ask more than one sandbox question per conversation, or ask sandbox questions in more than one conversation per day. But make sure you get at least one per day. After a week of this, it should feel more natural to use these questions all the time.

Quest Rewards:

- Easier to connect with others
- More interesting conversations
- Opportunity to learn about others

Side Quests:

- Write down a list of "sandbox" questions that are universally applicable. Memorize a few and have them ready for your next conversation.

- Ask yourself some "sandbox" questions and "linear" questions, and answer them as if you were in a real conversation. Get a feel for how the different questions prompt different responses. (Note: If you ask yourself a sandbox question and you don't know how to answer it, others may not know how to answer it either, so consider changing it.)

- Try to build a combo! In your conversations, practice asking sandbox questions that build on previous sandbox questions. For instance, if you ask someone "What do you like about your job?" and they reply "I like my coworkers—we have a lot of fun together" you might ask them, "What is your favorite memory with your coworkers?"

Stage Three: Looking For Group

Looking For Group Level One
ET The Extra Terrestrial

In 1983, the video game maker Atari—at one point the fastest growing company in America—lost over half a billion dollars (1.5 billion in today's dollars.) They shed more than a third of their workforce, and went into a tailspin from which they never recovered. The company was eventually split into pieces and sold to different buyers, and their destruction was so massive that it contributed to the entire U.S gaming industry entering a deep recession (known as the Video Game Crash of 1983.)

There were multiple reasons for Atari's implosion. The video game market at the time was heavily saturated, with a massive number of companies producing competing consoles. Game quality was often low, with many games produced by companies primarily as marketing tools. For instance, the Purina dog food company made a game promoting its dog food—as you might expect, it was not a very good game.

But one of the biggest reasons for the implosion was a single game: ET The Extra Terrestrial. The movie version of ET had been released earlier that year, and it was a smash hit. Atari smelled an opportunity and spent millions to buy the licensing rights to ET. Then they whipped together a game in just six weeks, and printed millions of cartridges in anticipation of massive sales.

The thing is, games that are made in just six weeks don't tend to be good games. And ET was no exception. In fact, it's considered one of the worst games of all time. Atari spent millions on a popular license, produced millions of game cartridges, and dropped a ton of money into marketing and promotion. But ET ended up being such a flop that Atari buried their excess cartridges in a New Mexico landfill.

It didn't matter how much Atari wanted ET to be a success, or how much they were willing to invest in marketing. Some games are just impossible to make successful.

The same thing is true of friendships. Some people just don't want to be your friend. Maybe they have enough friends, or maybe they're really busy, or maybe they just aren't interested. No matter how much

69

time you invest in pursuing these people, you're rarely going to see any positive results.

Worse, some people are happy to spend time with you, but they'll treat you poorly. They accept your invites to hang out, but they're rude to you, they don't respect your decisions, and they make you feel crummy. Every minute you spend with these toxic individuals will make your life worse.

Think of these people as "ET friends." An ET friend is someone who is a waste of your time and effort. That doesn't mean that they're a terrible person or that you should consider them an enemy—it just means that nothing good is likely to happen if you attempt to befriend them.

Unfortunately, it's easy to find yourself investing lots of time and energy into an ET friend. Maybe they lead you on, giving you the impression that they're interested even though they never actually accept your invites. Or maybe you don't have a lot of friends, and it's difficult to say no to hanging out with someone even if they treat you poorly. Or perhaps they were a good friend to you earlier, but now they treat you poorly or don't return your calls. Before you know it, you've invested weeks or months pursuing a friendship with someone and have very little to show for it. And because you've invested so much time chasing the ET friend, you haven't put as much time into building friendships with other people. It's a bad pattern to be caught in.

Fortunately, there's a simple solution. When you catch yourself wasting your time and effort with an ET friend, find someone else to spend time with!

If you've invited someone to hang out several times and they turn you down each time, invite someone else. If someone disrespects and belittles you every time you hang out, stop hanging out with them. Hang out with people who will be good friends to you instead.

Of course, just because someone is an ET friend today doesn't mean that you should avoid them forever. They might be ignoring you because they're super busy, or they might be rude to you because of problems in their personal life. If they used to be a good friend to you, you might try asking them why things have changed, and see if you can repair the relationship. Or if they were never a good friend to you, you might try cautiously reconnecting with them after a few months and see if their behavior has changed.

But until you see evidence that things are better, you should be very careful about investing lots of your time and energy into an ET friendship. Focus on people who are likely to be good friends instead.

Quest 3.1 (Type: Collection)

Quest Objectives

- Write down an inventory of the people that you consider your friends, or people you are trying to befriend. Ask yourself the following questions about each person:
- Does this person treat me and others well?
- Does this person seem like they want to spend time with me?
- Do I like spending time with this person?
- If the answer to any of those questions is "No", think about that relationship with that person.

Quest Description:

This quest is a bit touchy-feely, but give it a try. I think you might find it helpful.

Your goal here is to honestly look at your friendships and ask yourself if they are good and healthy. If they are, then awesome!

But if you realize that some of your relationships have serious problems, then perhaps you need to take action. Perhaps there is some conflict you need to resolve, or perhaps you are not being a very good friend to them and need to change your behavior. It's also possible that you've found one of your "ET friends", and the best response is for you to start spending less time with them.

Quest Rewards:

- More insight into your relationships
- The opportunity to improve your friendships or find new, better ones.
- It looks pretty cool to think deep thoughts while staring into the distance.

Side Quests:

- Take a few minutes to write down the best and worst friendships that you've had in the past. With the benefit of hindsight, try to identify what made the best friendships so good, and what made the worst friendships so bad. You may be able to identify some patterns that will help you avoid "ET friends" in your life today.

- Return to the list of your friends that you wrote down in the quest. This time, ask the questions of yourself. "Do I treat this person and others well?" "Do I act like I want to spend time with this person?" "Am I fun for this person to hang out with?" If any of the answers are "no", then try to find a solution so you can be a better friend.

- If you find that many of your friendships seem to be "ET" friends, talk about your friendships with a trusted family member or therapist. Some advice and encouragement could help you get on a path to better friendships.

Looking For Group Level Two
Consistency Makes The Clan

My freshman year of high school, I bought the last copy of Tribes 2 off a dusty shelf at a game store. It turned out to be one of the best gaming decisions I've ever made.

It wasn't just that I had a blast playing Tribes 2—although I did. Tribes 2 was essentially capture the flag with jetpacks (and tanks, and sniper rifles, and a gun called the spinfusor that shot blue exploding disks). It was easy for enemies to kill you unless you moved quickly, so the game required you to get extremely good at maintaining momentum as you flew across the battlefield. If you slowed down, you were dead. It was a mix of Battlefield, Titanfall, and Team Fortress—with a bit of gotta-go-fast Sonic thrown in for good measure. The gameplay was fast-paced and unique, and I loved it.

But the gameplay of Tribes 2 wasn't the best part. The best part for me, was my clan: Indiana Vehicles. I'll be the first to admit that "Indiana Vehicles" is not the best name to strike fear into the heart of our enemies, but the clan's founders lived in Indiana and they liked driving the vehicles in the game, so that's the clan name they picked.

Being a part of Indiana Vehicles was a fantastic experience for me. As a socially awkward freshman in high school, it was incredible to have a group where I belonged. To this day, I remember one of the other players posting a congratulatory message for me in our clan forums after I had performed a game-winning move in a close competitive match. My clan was more than teammates—they were friends.

But here's the thing. Those friendships only formed because we spent time together. Consistency was the glue that built our clan. Every Friday night, we would log on and game together. Every Friday, we would get to know each other a little more, we would make a few new memories, and our friendships would become a bit stronger.

And eventually, lack of consistency made the clan drift apart. People moved on to new games, fewer and fewer folks came to the Friday night practices, and eventually the whole thing shut down. I'm no longer in touch with anyone from that clan.

As you might imagine, this story has implications for your social journey. Two, to be exact.

First, you need to commit to a social group in order to make friends there. If you go to a group twice a year, you'll struggle to make friends there. But if you commit to going to every meeting you can for the next few months, you'll get to know people, and relationships will begin to form.

Of course, if you've gone to several meetings of a particular group and you hate it, you can stop going. But then find another group to commit to! A good rule of thumb is to try a new group every time you stop going to an old group, so that your total number of weekly social outings stays constant.

Second, you need to invest time in your friendships. If I had continued gaming with some clan mates after the clan disbanded, they might still be friends today. But because I didn't invest in those relationships, we lost touch.

So spend time with your friends. If they're local, ask them to see a movie, or grab lunch. If they're not living near you, give them a call every few months to catch up, or send them an email to say hi. If you consistently reach out to your friends, your friendship will grow.

Quest 3.2 (Type: Monthly)

Quest Objectives:

- Pick a social group you'd like to belong to (like a meetup group, a club, etc.)

- Commit to going to at least one meeting a week, four weeks in a row.

- Go to the SAME group four weeks in a row. No skipping around!

Quest Description:

I've asked you to do a similar quest in "Go Into The Tall Grass." But the difference here is commitment. With "Go Into The Tall Grass", you could visit a different group every week if you like. For this quest, you're stuck with one group for a month.

Of course, if you visit a group once or twice and you absolutely hate it, then you don't need to go back. But if you decide to quit a particular group, you need to start from the beginning with another group. That way you make sure you see the benefits of commitment.

Quest Rewards:

- Greater chance of making friends

- See the value of commitment

- Become a regular somewhere!

Side Quests:

- Plan an event that repeats monthly or weekly, and invite your friends to it. For instance, you might plan a monthly movie night, or a weekly game night. Run the event a few weeks or months in a row, and see if you can build up a group of regulars. If nobody comes the first time, that's okay—try again next week.

- Make a list of friends that you haven't talked to in a while. Then, call one friend on that list each week. (Consistency!)

- Try out Tribes for yourself! You can download Tribes 2 for free at TribesNext.com, although it's difficult to find a populated server these days. A better option might be to play Tribes Ascend, which is a modern sequel to Tribes 2 that keeps many of the same gameplay elements (it's free to play on Steam.)

Looking For Group Level Three
Go Karting With Bowser

Mario and Bowser have a weird relationship. While they started as arch-enemies, they ended up as...friends?

Ben Cronshaw (Yahtzee from "Zero Punctuation") sums it up pretty well:

"For me, the interesting relationship is the one between Mario and Bowser; I mean on some days they fight to the death in fiery climactic showdowns, while on other days they go go-karting together, play tennis, even team up in some of the RPGs. Sure, he kidnaps the Princess a whole bunch, but no-one seems to begrudge him for that anymore; it's just what he does."

This strange relationship has led to a TV Trope called "Go Karting With Bowser." It's this idea that despite starting as enemies, Mario and Bowser have spent so much time together in so many different contexts that they've grown to have something approaching friendship.

Obviously, this is just an idea. It's never been expressed in the games themselves (although Mario and Bowser do show a grudging respect for each other when they ally together in games like Super Mario RPG.) But the idea makes sense. After all, if you spend a lot of time with someone, in a lot of different contexts, it's natural that a friendship would form.

You can put the same principle to work in your own life as you try to make new friends. I'm not recommending that you invite your worst enemy to go go-karting together (they would probably say no and look at you strangely.) Instead, apply the "Go-Karting with Bowser" technique to people who are not your enemies, but who aren't your friends yet, either.

This is what the Go-Karting With Bowser technique boils down to: Spend time with someone outside of the original context where you met them. Bowser and Mario met as arch-rivals battling for the Princess, but then they started playing tennis, racing go-karts, teaming up in RPGs, etc. By spending time together outside of the original context, they were able to see a new side of each other, and friendship was able to form.

In your life, the same principle holds true. Let's say you meet someone at work. You get along well, but you never spend time together outside of work. If you invite them to do something together outside of work, then you get to see a new side of them—you can see who they are when they're not working, when they don't have to behave in front of the boss, when they can relax. Hanging out with someone in multiple contexts helps the two of you to get to know each other better, and this makes friendship more likely to spark.

Also, inviting someone to spend time together outside of the original context sends a strong signal that you are interested in friendship with them. Let's say you frequently go to a board gaming meetup, and you enjoy playing games with a particular person while you're there. That person doesn't know if you like them as a person, or if you just like playing games with them. But if you invite them to do something outside of the gaming group, you are signaling to them that you think they're a cool person. They know that you want to hang out with them, not just play games with them. That gives them the encouragement they need to start inviting you to do stuff with them, too.

Of course, this strategy (like all other strategies in this book) requires some consistency. If you invite a coworker to hang out outside of work once, and then never invite them to do anything ever again, a friendship is unlikely to form. But there is a nice snowball effect that happens. If you start inviting someone to do things together, then they will usually start inviting you to do things together too. That makes the friendship easy to grow and maintain.

Quest 3.3 (Type: Collection)

Quest Objectives:

- Use the Go-Karting With Bowser technique on three different people.

Quest Description:

Find three people who you get along well with, but you only know in one context. Invite each of them (one at a time) to do something together outside of the original context. Maybe you ask someone from your meetup group to see a movie together, or maybe you ask a classmate if they want to come over for some gaming. If you don't have three people that come to mind, spend a few weeks visiting some social groups to build some connections (or just ask one or two people to start.)

You should also try to pick an invitation that you think the other person will like. If you know your coworker is outdoorsy, invite them to go hiking together. If someone from your Meetup group loves music, invite them to a concert. If you're not sure, pick something that most people will enjoy, like a fun movie. A good way to find ideas is to Google for "fun things to do in [your city]."

One word of warning: Be careful if you're asking someone of the opposite sex to do something together one on one, since that might be construed as romantic instead of friendly. If your intentions are purely friendly, you might want to let them know it's just a friendly invite, or invite them to a group event instead. I would also steer clear of dinner-and-a-movie or other traditional date ideas.

Remember, if they say no, that's okay! You can wait a few weeks and invite them to something else, or you can just ask another person. People won't always say yes to invitations, but they will usually appreciate being asked. Even if they didn't accept your invitation, you still signaled a desire for friendship, and that counts for something.

Quest Rewards:

- Greater social confidence

- Opportunity for fun experiences
- Make some new friends!

Side Quests:

- Plan a group event that would be fun for multiple people that you know. Invite all of them. That way you can get to know them better, and they can also potentially make friends with each other!

- If someone is already your friend but you only spend time together in a few different contexts, add a new context to the mix. For instance, if you have a friend but the only thing you do together is video games and movie nights, try inviting them to go bowling together and see if they are interested.

- Invite someone over to play Mario Kart or Mario Party. That way you can literally be Go-Karting with Bowser as you use the Go-Karting with Bowser technique!

Looking For Group Level Four
Speedrunning Gone Home

Gone Home is a work of art.

It tells the story of a young woman who arrives home and finds it deserted. You guide her as she explores her abandoned house and pieces together the story of what happened to her family. Polygon awarded the game a perfect 10, and the coveted Game of the Year award.

It's gorgeous, immersive, and deeply moving. If you take the time to deeply explore every nook and cranny of the house, you'll be richly rewarded with a story that stays with you long after the credits roll.

Or, you can speed run it in about 90 seconds.

Grab the first key, go to a secret room, grab the second key, go to the last room, win the game. Easy.

Of course, you miss the story, the emotion, and the deep immersion. In other words, you've missed everything that makes Gone Home, Gone Home.

It's a fun challenge, of course. But if all you ever do is speedrun, you missed the point.

A friendship should be like playing Gone Home. Gone Home is a game of exploration, where your curiosity is gradually rewarded by learning more and more about your lost family. The more time you spend looking for clues, the more you'll discover.

Friendship is a game of exploration too. If your friends see that you want to get to know them, they'll start to open up to you. The more you show a genuine interest in them, the more they'll share.

Ask them how they're doing, and they'll tell you. Show interest in their past and they'll tell you stories. Earn their trust and they'll share their deep fears and dreams. Give it time, and they'll start showing genuine interest in you, too.

But you have to ask. You have to show interest. You have to let them know that you care.

And most people don't. Most people "speedrun" their conversations. This is what someone speedrunning a conversation looks like:

- Instead of showing curiosity in the other person's life, they only talk about themselves.
- Instead of picking meaningful topics, they talk only about video games, sports or another hobby.
- Instead of asking follow-up questions when someone shares something personal, they change the topic.
- Instead of giving the other person their full attention, they look at their phone.

You can think of it this way:

Speedrunning a conversation is when you talk only about superficial things, and don't show a genuine interest in the other person. You stop speedrunning when you give the other person your full attention, and show a genuine curiosity about their life. The easiest way to show this genuine curiosity is to ask questions about the person's feelings, passions, or life experiences. For instance:

- How are you feeling about the test that's coming up this week? (feelings)
- If you could do anything as a career, what would it be? (passions)
- What did you do this summer? (life experiences?)

Note that most people will probably give a superficial answer the first time you ask a question like this, so you usually need to ask a follow-up question to show that you're really interested. For instance:

You:
"How are you feeling about the test that's coming up this week?"

Them:
"A little stressed, I guess." (a superficial answer)

You:
> "What are you most stressed about?" (a follow up question that shows interest.)

Them:
> "Well, it's the essay portion. I'm not a very good writer, so I feel…." (and they give a real answer).

Of course, speedrunning a conversation doesn't make you a bad person or a bad friend. Everyone does it sometimes. But you're not going to deepen your friendship unless you take the time to really get to know the other person.

Here's an easy way to tell if you're speedrunning a conversation. Ask yourself:

- Is the other person telling me how they feel? (not just what they think.)
- Is the other person telling me something important about them that I don't know?
- Is the other person talking about something they are truly passionate about?
- Is the other person telling me a story from their life?

If the answer to all four of those questions is "No", you're probably speedrunning—and you should ask some questions to show interest in the other person.

Quest 3.4 (Type: Daily)

Quest Objectives:

- For one week, keep a daily log of your conversations with friends. Mark if each conversation was speedrunning or exploration.

- At the end of the week, review the log. Check how often you speedrun.

Quest Description:

When you review the log, count up the number of "speedrun" conversations where you only talk about superficial things, and count up the number of "exploration" conversations, where you ask questions and show a genuine interest. See if you can get at least one exploration conversation each day.

This log doesn't need to be fancy. Basically, I just want you to start noticing if your conversations are superficial or if you're going deeper. A simple piece of paper or Google doc should be just fine. Try to track any conversation that lasts more than a minute or two, but it's okay if you skip very short interactions.

Quest Rewards:

- Better conversations

- A deeper sense of connection with others

- Make others feel appreciated

Side Quests:

- Play Gone Home! Just don't speedrun it :)

- Spend fifteen minutes coming up with a list of questions that you can use to show a genuine interest in people. You might try to brainstorm on your own, or Google for ideas ("conversation starters" is usually a good place to start.)

- Notice when another person makes you feel like they are showing a genuine interest in you. Pay attention to what they do to make you feel that way, and try to do the same things to someone else.

Looking For Group Level Five
Left 4 Dead

I have spent at least 200 hours playing the Left 4 Dead series.

I say "at least" because I started playing Left 4 Dead before Steam started tracking game time, so my total number is probably even higher.

To put this time in context, instead of playing Left 4 Dead, I could have listed to War and Peace on audiobook—three times in a row. I could have flown around the world four times, and collected an epic collection of airline peanuts along the way. I could have completed the 200 hours of training necessary to become a certified yoga instructor (only to flunk out when they discovered I can't touch my toes). But instead I spend 200+ hours shooting zombies.

And I don't regret a minute of it.

See, Left 4 Dead wasn't just a game to me. It was a way to make memories with my friends. When you're standing shoulder to shoulder with three of your buddies, facing down a zombie horde—well, there's nothing quite like it.

Now, coop gaming wasn't revolutionary even back in 2008, and Left 4 Dead was not the first game that pit a team of players against a slavering horde. DOOM (released back in 1993) came with a coop feature. And like most kids that grew up on the Super Nintendo, I had spent many hours fighting alongside a friend in games like TMNT: Turtles In Time. So what was so captivating about Left 4 Dead?

Simple. Left 4 Dead was the first game where you truly needed your friends. In other coop games before L4D, a skilled player could beat the game all by themselves. It certainly helped to have a partner, but if you were good enough, you could handle all the enemies on your own.

But in Left 4 Dead, you need your teammates. See, Left 4 Dead features powerful enemies called the "Special Infected." Most Special Infected have attacks that render you completely helpless almost instantly. One moment you're running along, guns blazing, and the next moment you've got a Hunter pinning you down and seconds to live before he shreds you to pieces. The only way you can escape a Special Infected's clutches is if a teammate arrives to rescue you.

So you learn to stay close to your allies. You learn to keep tabs on them, and make sure they're okay. You learn to communicate constantly, sharing strategies and information. And most of all, you learn to ask for help—quickly!

When this happens, the experience is amazing. See, you're not just playing a game anymore. You're part of a team. It's immersive, exhilarating, and the stuff that legendary gaming memories are made of.

And it's all built on needing your teammates, and knowing that they need you.

Great friendships are built on the same thing. Another way to say "a great group of friends" is to say "A group of people who know they need each other."

Take me, for instance. I don't need my friends every day. Most of the time, my friendships revolve around having fun together. But when the chips are down, when I'm at the end of my rope—I know I don't have to do it alone. I know my friends are there to help. And my friends know I'll be there for them when they need me.

This might sound weird, because many people think it's weak to need other people. And sure, you don't need people in the sense that you'll wither up and die without good friends. But if you want to live life to the fullest, you need good friends.

You need friends who can remind you of your values and their goals, and encourage you not to compromise on the things they believe in. You need friends who can help cheer you up when you're in a bad mood, or comfort you when life is hard. You need friends who can broaden your horizons, and show your new amazing things about life.

It's not weak to need these things. It's human.

And you don't just need these things. You deserve them. That's part of being human, too.

And here's the thing—other people need this too. And you can give it. You can be the person who believes in someone until they achieve their dreams. You can be the person who makes someone smile for the first time in a week. You can be the person who gives someone else their first taste of true friendship.

This is my point. It's fantastic to spend time with your friends hanging out and having fun. But if you don't learn to lean on each other, you're missing out on the full power of friendship.

I know that phrases like "the full power of friendship" make me sound like a starry-eyed Brony, but trust me—once you've experienced what I'm talking about, you'll understand why I'm so passionate. Giving you that experience is what this quest is all about.

Quest 3.5 (Type: Collection)

Quest Objectives:

- Practice needing someone, twice.

Quest Description

The easiest way to do this is to find someone who is good at a skill that you are bad at. Then, ask that person to teach you how to do that skill.

For instance, if you're terrible in the kitchen, ask your friend who loves cooking to help you make a great dinner. If you're afraid of the weight room, ask your athlete friend to show you how to bench press. If you've never picked up a guitar before, ask your musician friend to help you play a few notes.

Of course, you're not going to become an expert in any of these skills in one lesson. But that's not the point. The point is that you will experience being dependent on your friend. You will be fumbling, you will be needy—and you will be okay. You'll get to overcome the discomfort of relying on someone else, and you'll also get to experience the thrill of achieving something you couldn't do on your own.

Then the next time you really need to rely on a friend, you'll remember that it's okay to need people, and you'll be more likely to reach out. That's a great reward.

Quest Rewards:

- Make a meaningful memory with a friend
- Learn a new skill
- Become more comfortable with relying on others.

Side Quests:

- Ask a friend for advice on a problem that you are having.

- If you have a friend who is struggling in some area, ask them if there is anything you can do to help.

- Get three other friends together and play a 4-player game of Left 4 Dead!

Looking For Group Level Six
The Sims

I used to have a love-hate relationship with The Sims.

I would love starting a new game of The Sims. I'd spend a long time designing my avatar to look like me, then I'd plop him into a new house and start navigating the tricky financial decisions of a new Sim (protip: save money on a dishwasher by hiding your dirty dishes in the front yard!)

The next few hours would pass in a happy blur as I started a career, made a few friends, and settled into a routine. But pretty soon, I found myself bored and frustrated.

See, once I'd passed the early stages of the game and found a good career, my game would quickly devolve into a tedious three-step process:

1. Wake up, go to work.

2. Come home, build my Sim's happiness up to the bare minimum needed to perform well at work, and grind skills until nighttime.

3. Go to bed and repeat step 1.

While this was profitable for my Sim, it wasn't very much fun for me. So inevitably, I would end up quitting in frustration (only to return a few months later when The Sims itch struck again.)

This lasted until I had an epiphany: I had been trying to win The Sims. And The Sims isn't made to be won. It was made to be enjoyed.

When I realized this, The Sims became much more fun. I stopped trying to climb the career ladder or do everything "right." Instead, I became playful and creative.

I tried lots of fun experiments. Could a family of teenagers living with no adults survive on pizza and part time jobs? How many people could my Sim fall in love with? What if my Sim has AS MANY BABIES AS POSSIBLE?

The result? I started having fun with The Sims again. Instead of trying to climb the corporate ladder, I was letting my imagination run free. Instead of worrying about optimizing my Sim's performance, I let myself write a story with them. Instead of trying to rack up the Simoleans, I made AS MANY BABIES AS POSSIBLE.

I had a similar epiphany with my friendships.

See, for a long time I was a social outcast. And even after I started to make friends, I still felt like I didn't belong. I felt like I was an imposter, and feared that my friends would reject me if they knew how awkward I really was. I was worried that if I made any social mistake at all, that my friends would turn their backs on me. I would be alone again.

So I treated my friendships like a competitive game that I had to win. Instead of focusing on having fun together, I focused on avoiding social mistakes. Instead of showing my real self to my friends, I gave a sugarcoated version of myself that hid my flaws.

Needless to say, this was exhausting. And eventually, I learned it was unnecessary. I learned that my friends didn't mind if I made a social mistake. I learned that my friends weren't afraid of my flaws, and I saw how much they appreciated me just being myself. I stopped treating my friendships as something that I needed to win, and I started treating them as something to enjoy.

And not only has that reduced my stress considerably, but it's also made me a better friend. After all, would you rather spend your time with someone who trusts you enough to be real with you, or would you rather be with someone who was afraid of your judgement? I think most people would prefer to be with someone who trusts them.

Of course, trust is earned. There's a time and a place for you to be your real self, and there's a time and a place for you to be more filtered. It's probably a good idea to work on making a good impression during a job interview or a first date.

But with your good friends, you can stop worrying about winning. They already like you. You don't need to impress them, and you don't to be flawless. Just be you. Focus on enjoying the friendship, allow your real self to show—and then sit back and see what happens.

Quest 3.6 (Type: Collection)

Quest Objectives:

Take a few minutes and write down an answer to these questions:

1. If I was completely focused on impressing my friends and 'winning' our interactions, how would I behave?

2. If I was completely focused on enjoying my time with my friends and being my real self, how would I behave?

After you write down your answers, ask yourself which one sounds more like the way you normally behave.

Quest Description:

This quest is all about introspection, so do it in whatever way feels best to you. You might just write down some bullet points for each answer, or you could write a paragraph if that feels more natural.

Once you finish with your answers, take time to reflect. Do you act more like you're trying to impress your friends and avoid social mistakes, or more like you're trying to enjoy your friendships and be yourself?

Then, ask yourself why. And ask yourself if there's anything you need to do to change that.

Quest Rewards:

- Better insight into your relationships
- Opportunity to make needed changes.
- The chance to live a life that's more in line with your goals.

Side Quests:

- If you find that you are normally focused on "winning" interactions, spend a day trying to enjoy your interactions. See what happens.

- If you own a copy of The Sims, spend an evening playing creatively, without worrying about winning or achieving objectives.

- Read "Alice and Kev" (aliceandkev.wordpress.com). It's a phenomenal example of the kind of storytelling that's possible when you're not trying to win The Sims.

Looking For Group Level Seven
Modding

During its heyday, the original StarCraft was flooded with an amazing variety of custom user created maps. While some maps were designed to be used in a typical StarCraft match, many of the custom maps pushed the limits of StarCraft's scripting engine to provide gameplay that was completely new. There were RPGs where your character leveled over time, tower defense games where you fended off hordes of enemies, even maps that let you play chess and soccer within StarCraft.

I would play these custom maps endlessly as a kid. And one day, I decided to make my own.

I had no scripting or mapmaking experience, and I was about twelve at the time. So the deck was stacked against me. But that didn't hold me back. I poured hours into StarCraft's mapmaker, and eventually emerged with my masterpiece: StarCraft Rock Paper Scissors (StarCraft RPS for short.)

Okay, so maybe "masterpiece" is too strong of a word. But it was a darn good map, and I'm still proud of what I was able to accomplish.

I set up the map so that players would move their initial unit to one of three beacons, choosing rock, paper or scissors. Depending on their choice, they would then warp in a battle cruiser, a goliath, or a firebat (For those of you who haven't played StarCraft: a battle cruiser is a spaceship, a goliath is a guy in a robot suit, and a firebat is a guy with a flamethrower.)

I set up the units' weapons so the battle cruiser killed the firebat, the firebat killed the goliath, and the goliath killed the battle cruiser. The outcome was always inevitable, but the losing player could add some excitement by running around and trying to dodge the winning player. It was a pretty clever design, if I do say so myself.

Now, nobody is still playing StarCraft RPS today, nor did Blizzard ever offer me a job. But that map still sticks out in my memory, because StarCraft RPS was my first opportunity to really give back to the gaming community. I had been enjoying games that other people had made since I first got my hands on a controller. But now I could finally give someone else the enjoyment that games had given me.

It was thrilling to play a game of StarCraft RPS with someone, and have them come back for a rematch. They had an entire ocean of custom games to play, and were choosing to play mine—again and again. That experience of giving back is one of my fondest StarCraft memories.

Since you've made it this far in the book, you know the social application is just around the corner. And this time, I'm going to give you a challenge.

If you're like most of my readers, your goal in reading this book was to become more socially confident, and develop a great group of friends. And that is a fantastic goal, and I hope you achieve it.

But I also hope you don't stop there.

See, there's lots of people in the world still looking for that group of friends. There's lots of people who don't have many friends, who worry they don't fit in, who would absolutely love it if you invited them to hang out sometime.

So invite them to hang out.

It's pretty easy—just keep your eyes open for folks that look like they need a friend. And then be a friend to them.

Ask if they'd like to grab lunch or see a movie sometime. Invite them along next time you plan a group event. Strike up a conversation next time you see them. Of course, sometimes they'll turn you down. Maybe they prefer solitude, or maybe you just don't click together. But if you keep being friendly towards folks who need a friend, you'll find others who accept your invitations with enthusiasm.

This shouldn't be a charity project. Most of the time folks who don't have many friends are actually pretty awesome—they just need someone to give them the chance. So if you reach out, you'll be rewarded.

Some of my best gaming memories came from sharing StarCraft RPS with others. I hope you'll find that some of your best friends come from the people you reached out to.

Quest 3.7 (Type: Collection)

Quest Objectives:

- Deliberately reach out to ten people

Quest Description:

Yes, that's a lot. But this is the last quest of the book, so I think you're up to the challenge.

When you think about folks who might appreciate a new friend, are there any specific people who come to mind? If so, your quest is pretty simple – just invite those people to spend time with you. Start with one, and build from there.

If nobody comes to mind, then your quest has two parts.

1. Keep your eyes open. Try to look for people standing by themselves during social gatherings, or folks who never seem to have any plans for the weekend. You might also keep your eyes peeled for people who look sad or anxious. Or just look for the folks who mention that they're interested in hanging out and making new friends!

2. Reach out. Strike up a conversation and try to establish some common interests. If there's a connection, consider inviting them to hang out sometime.

Technically, once you've reached out to ten people, this quest is complete. But out of all of the quests in the book, I think this is the best one to never stop doing.

Make this a lifelong quest. Keep your eyes permanently peeled for folks who are in need of friends, and do your best to be a good friend to them.

If you do, you will make a huge difference in the world—and you will be rewarded with an amazing group of friends.

Quest Rewards:

- Make a big impact in the lives of others
- Create meaningful friendships
- Build connections wherever you go.

Side Quests:

- Has anyone ever reached out to you? Maybe someone befriended you when you felt lonely, or gave you a listening ear when you needed support. If so, send them a thank-you email or phone call.

- After you've reached out to a few different people, plan some kind of event and invite all of them. Spark some friendships between your new friends!

- Write down a description of the kind of friend you want. Then be that friend to other people.

Appendix 1: Cheat Codes

At the back of any good strategy guide are the cheat codes.

These "cheat codes" are quick social skills tips that are easy to learn and easy to apply. They're not cheats in the sense of being sneaky or underhanded—everything here is ethical. But just like a cheat code is easy to use but has a big impact on your game, these social cheat codes are easy to learn and have the potential to really help you out.

Eye Contact

It's important to give the right amount of eye contact. Too much, and people think you're staring at them—which is creepy and weird. Too little, and you come across as dishonest and shy.

But how much is the right amount? And how do you keep track of your eye contact when you are already focusing on all of the other parts of the conversation?

There's two rules of thumb that I find work pretty well. Try both and see which one works better for you.

The first rule of thumb is to **look at them when one of you is talking, and look away when you are thinking**. This is what I normally do, and it usually creates the right balance of looking towards and looking away. I also find it helpful to break eye contact when I'm thinking, since it helps me concentrate.

If that doesn't work for you, a second rule of thumb is to **give the other person about the same amount of eye contact they give you**. That means you should look at them when they look at you, and look away when they look away.

Of course, if you look away at the exact instant the other person looks away, they'll probably notice you are copying them. So I recommend you follow the other person but with a delay. If they look at you, wait a moment or two and then look at them. If they look away, keep looking at them for a few seconds and then let your gaze drift away.

No matter which rule of thumb you pick, remember that you don't need a precise amount of eye contact—you just need to be in the right ballpark. So don't worry about following these rules perfectly. If you make a reasonable effort, you should be in the right ballpark.

Posture

Good posture is important in social situations. Standing up straight with your shoulders back creates an air of confidence, which helps you create a positive impression on others. Plus, some research indicates that when your body language is confident, you start to feel more confident, too.

But if you're like most gamers, your posture is not the best. So how do you fix your posture?

Well, there's no easy fix for permanently fixing your posture. If you want good posture for the long term, you had better talk to a physical therapist and embark on an exercise regimen to strengthen your back.

However, there is a pretty easy way to temporarily give yourself good posture—it only lasts a few minutes, but that's enough to make a positive impression.

In order to instantly improve your posture, **imagine there is a cup of freezing cold water on your head and it's about to spill**. If you're like most people, this imagination will automatically cause you to stand up straight, pull your head back and straighten your shoulders so that you walk straight. You'll maintain this posture as long as you keep imagining the cup of water on your head.

You can test this if you like—just walk up to a mirror the way you normally do, then walk up to a mirror while imagining the cup of water. You should notice a difference in how you look and move. If not, feel free to imagine something else that changes your posture. For instance, you might imagine that you are wearing an antigravity helmet that pulls your head up, or you might imagine you are wearing a suit of armor that prevents you from hunching over.

Again, this only lasts as long as you remember to actively imagine the cup of water. But if you imagine the cup of water right before you walk into a social setting, you can give yourself a posture and confidence boost that should give you big benefits.

Motivating Yourself To Be Social

There's a simple trick from psychology for motivating yourself to be more social.

It's usually used in the world of sales. Instead of asking "Do you want to buy a car?" a salesmen will ask "Would you rather buy the red car or the blue car?" No matter which you choose, you still end up buying a car.

It's also used by parents, who ask their kids "Do you want carrots or broccoli with dinner?" instead of "Do you want to eat vegetables with dinner?" Rather than giving their kids the chance to say no, they only give their kids options that lead to healthy veggies.

You can use this trick with yourself, too. **If you have a choice to be social or non-social, instead make it a choice between two social options.** In other words, instead of asking "Should I go to that party on Friday night?", find another social opportunity for Friday night, and choose between those two.

For instance, you might think "Oh, there's a new cool movie out—I could ask a friend to see that on Friday." So now your choice is between watching the movie and going to the party, which are both good social options, instead of the party or doing nothing social.

This also works when you are already at a social setting. For instance, let's say you're at a party but you aren't talking to anyone. Instead of thinking "Should I start a conversation or not?", try asking yourself "Should I start a conversation with this person or with that person?" or "Should I join that group by the snack bar, or that group that's playing Guitar Hero?" No matter what you choose, you'll move towards more social opportunities.

There are two important caveats for this trick, though.

First, it is okay to be non-social sometimes. If you've had a rough week and you really need to give yourself some quality alone time, don't force yourself to be social. Or if you are at a party but you're feeling exhausted, it's fine to take some time to just people watch and recharge. But if you do want to motivate yourself to be more social, this is a helpful trick.

Second, avoid using this trick on other people. While you can occasionally nudge people's behavior by asking them to choose between two options instead of choosing yes or no, you can also come across as rude and pushy.

For instance, if you ask a stranger "Will you go on a date with me?" you're likely to get rejected (since they don't know you.) If you ask a stranger "Would you like to go on a date with me to a restaurant, or on a date with me to a movie?" you're still likely to get rejected, and you're likely to offend the stranger (because you were obviously trying to manipulate them into doing something they wouldn't normally do.)

Third, this only works if the options you give yourself are reasonable. If you think, "Should I talk to 100 strangers at a bar, or call up every single one of my friends?" you will still end up saying "No!" to both options. So choose options that, while potentially challenging, are still doable.

To sum up: Use this trick only when you are ready to be social (not when you truly need alone time), only on yourself (not others where it can be manipulative), and only with reasonable options.

Memorizing Names

Your social success will increase quite a bit once you master the art of memorizing names. If you know someone's name, it's easier to get their attention and start a conversation with them. It's also super awkward when the other person realizes you've forgotten their name, especially if you've known them for weeks.

Fortunately, you don't need a fantastic memory to be great at memorizing names. All you need to do is follow three steps.

First, **repeat their name** as soon as you get it. So if they say, "Hey, my name is Felicia" you should immediately say, "Nice to meet you, Felicia."

You should also be deliberate to use their name a few times in the following conversation. The easiest way is to include it in a question "Anyway, Felicia, what do you do?" If you use it a few times, you're likely to remember it.

Second, **make their name memorable.** The easiest way to do this is by creating a nickname for them. To do this, combine their name with a word that starts with the same letter and that evokes a strong visual image. For instance, if you meet a Dave, immediately think "Dapper Dave." If you meet a Susan, immediately think "Sunny Susan."

These words don't really need to have anything to do with the person themselves, and they don't have to make much sense. It's perfectly fine to think "George the Giraffe" or "Crunchy Carl." The important thing is to come up with the nickname quickly, so use whatever first comes to mind.

The reason this works is because the pairing words are naturally memorable, since they create a strong image. So if you look at George, you'll naturally remember "Giraffe", and then you'll remember, "Ok, his name starts with a G...." and it will be much easier to remember "George." (Just make sure you don't call him George the Giraffe out loud.)

Third, **If you forget their name, ask for it as soon as reasonably possible**. Everyone forgets names sometimes, and there's no great shame in it. However, the longer you wait to ask for a reminder, the more awkward it becomes (have you ever gone weeks not knowing someone's name because you were afraid to ask for it again?) So if you realize you've forgotten someone's name, look for a graceful opportunity to ask for it again. They might need a reminder of your name, too!

So to sum up: Say their name out loud as soon as you hear it. Combine their name with a memorable word to create a nickname, and use the nickname to help you remember. And if you forget their name, ask them again as soon as you can (and do your best to remember this time!)

Stop Saying Words Like "Um" and "Like"

Um, sometimes when you're, like, talking, you can find yourself, ah, adding lots of extra, um, words that don't, like, mean anything.

These words are called filler words, and they're a bad habit. Generally, we use filler words when we need to pause for a moment to think of what to say next. It feels strange to just stop talking while you think of what to say, so you use a filler word to fill the silence. For example, you don't say "We need more [pause] potatoes", you say "We need more, um, potatoes."

The problem is that filler words are distracting and they make you appear less confident. Worse, you don't need them to fill the silence. It's totally fine to just pause for a moment to collect your thoughts. Search Youtube for "famous speeches" and listen to a few. You'll notice that the speakers pause frequently—instead of using filler words, they just stop talking for a moment when necessary.

So how do you get rid of filler words? Well, there's a technique I learned at a club called Toastmasters. Toastmasters is an organization that has groups all around the world that meet up to practice public speaking together. Because good public speakers don't use filler words, Toastmasters has developed a technique to train their members to avoid filler words. They call it the "Ah bell."

Essentially, when you are giving a speech and you use a filler word (like "ah"), someone in the audience will ring a loud, annoying bell. The bell noise is startling and annoying, and you quickly learn to avoid using filler words to protect yourself from the bell.

You can apply the same technique on your own. Just find a friend and give the friend an annoying bell (or squirt bottle that sprays cold water on you, or something else equally unpleasant.) Then hang out and talk as normal. Anytime you use a filler word, your friend can ring the bell or spray you with cold water. A few sessions of this and you will learn how to monitor your speech for filler words. (You can also just join Toastmasters!)

If you don't have any friends who are interested in doing this with you, you can do it by yourself. Find a list of questions online—for instance, search for "first date questions." Then answer each question out loud, just talking to your computer screen (make sure nobody else is around.) Each time you use a filler word, spray yourself with cold water, or snap a rubber band on your wrist, or something else shocking and unpleasant (but not harmful.) Of course, this is not as good as having a friend help you, since you might not catch every time you use a filler word. But if you practice this a few times, you should still see results. You can even record your answers on video and review the videos to track your progress.

And remember, you don't need to completely eliminate filler words from your speech. If you say "um" occasionally, it's not a big deal. But the goal is to use them very rarely. If your speech is mostly free of filler words, you'll appear much more confident and charismatic. Good luck!

Appendix 2: Achievements

As if writing a book on gaming wasn't nerdy enough, I've added achievements. If you're able to complete these—congrats!

Exclamation Point

Complete your first quest

Oh Baby A Triple!

Complete all three sidequests for a level.

A Winner Is You

Finish reading the whole book

Max Level

Complete all quests in the book

God Mode

Complete all quests and side quests

Warp Whistle

Read the book out of order.

Spectator Mode

Read the entire book without doing any quests. Note: This is a bad achievement to have :) Go and do the quests!

Respawn

Experience a social failure or setback. Keep going anyway.

Noclip Mode

Read this book on an airplane

Cross-Platform Gameplay

Buy at least two of the three formats of the guide (Ebook, printed book, and audiobook.)

Researcher

Play every game mentioned in this book.

Up-up-down-down-left-right-left-right-B-A

Use a technique from the cheat code appendix

Ready Player Two

Share this book with a friend

Speedrunner

Finish the entire book in one day.

Let's Play

Write a review of this book on Amazon

New Game +

Start the book again after you've read it once.

Retro Gamer

Read my first book, *Improve Your Social Skills*

Appendix 3: Where To Play Every Game Mentioned In This Book

Stage One

Level 1.4: Go Into The Tall Grass

Pokémon games: Buy them basically anywhere.

Level 1.5: Infinite lives

Don't Starve: Buy it on Steam or Gog.com

Level 1.6: Hardware

StarCraft and StarCraft 2: Buy them basically anywhere

Zombies Run: Zombiesrungame.com or search for it in the app store.

Hearthstone: Play it free at Battle.net

Level 1.7: It's Dangerous To Go Alone

Gordon Freeman is from the Half Life series, Link is from the Legend of Zelda series, and Mario is well, Mario. All of them are available basically everywhere.

Stage Two

Level 2.1: Pong

Pong: Play it at http://www.ponggame.org/

Level 2.2: Minecraft

Minecraft: Buy it basically everywhere.

Terraria: Buy it on Steam

Level 2.3: Parsers

Play the original King's Quest games for free at Sarien.net or buy them on Steam or Gog.com. Play the fan-made remakes for free at AGDInteractive.com, or buy the professional remakes on Steam. Lots of options!

Level 2.4: The Whelk

Final Fantasy Six: If you own a SNES or a Playstation 1, you can get the original version. Otherwise, you can buy a remake with some updated visuals on the iPhone or Android store, or on Steam.

Level 2.5: Noor The Pacifist

World of Warcraft: Battle.net or Amazon

Level 2.6 Turtling

StarCraft/StarCraft 2: Battle.net or Amazon.

Level 2.7 Sandbox

Skyrim, Minecraft and Grand Theft Auto: Buy them literally anywhere.

Stage Three

Level 3.1 ET: The Extra Terrestrial

It's not available for sale anywhere, but you can find it online by searching for "Play ET Game." Some of the sites offering it are a bit sketchy, so play at your own risk.

Level 3.2 Consistency Makes The Clan

Tribes 2 is available at TribesNext.com. You can also play the modern version of Tribes—Tribes Ascend—for free on Steam.

Level 3.4 Speedrunning Gone Home

Gone Home is available on Gog.com or Steam

Level 3.5 Left 4 Dead

Left 4 Dead and Left 4 Dead 2 are are available on Steam or Amazon.

Level 3.6 The Sims

You can buy the Sims pretty much anywhere, although the Sims 4 is not available on Steam (only Origin or at game retailers.)

Level 3.7 Modding

The original StarCraft can be purchased on Amazon or at Battle.net. If you'd like to play my Rock Paper Scissors map, you can download it at ImproveYourSocialSkills.com/StarCraft-Rock-Paper-Scissors

About the Author

Playing King's Quest as a kid   *Me today*

I'm Dan, and I like people.

A few things about me:

- I live in Portland, Oregon and am currently pursuing a doctorate in clinical psychology.

- I spoke at TEDx about "My Life With Asperger's." You can watch my talk at http://bit.ly/tedxdan.

- I'm the author of ImproveYourSocialSkills.com, and I offer social skills coaching to clients all around the world.

Thanks again for reading the book! The support from my readers has been nothing short of amazing, and I am deeply grateful for everyone who has journeyed with me to improve their social skills.

If you have any questions or comments, feel free to get in touch. Following the example of Mr. Rogers, I respond to everyone who contacts me, so don't hesitate to reach out. You can email me at Dan@ImproveYourSocialSkills.com or at DanielWendler.com.

Made in the USA
San Bernardino, CA
16 January 2017